Hear the Spirit

Hear the Spirit

ritual poems & radical litanies

RAEDORAH C. STEWART

RESOURCE *Publications* · Eugene, Oregon

HEAR THE SPIRIT
ritual poems & radical litanies

Copyright © 2025 Raedorah C. Stewart. All rights reserved. Except for brief quotations in critical publications or reviews, no part of this book may be reproduced in any manner without prior written permission from the publisher. Write: Permissions, Wipf and Stock Publishers, 199 W. 8th Ave., Suite 3, Eugene, OR 97401.

Resource Publications
An Imprint of Wipf and Stock Publishers
199 W. 8th Ave., Suite 3
Eugene, OR 97401

www.wipfandstock.com

PAPERBACK ISBN: 979-8-3852-3771-5
HARDCOVER ISBN: 979-8-3852-3772-2
EBOOK ISBN: 979-8-3852-3773-9
VERSION NUMBER 08/08/25

For all the pastors who have called on me,
the congregations I have served,
seminarians I have mentored, students I have taught,
and worship and arts committees who trust me to hear the Spirit.

Contents

Acknowledgments | xiii
Preface | xv

Invocations
Speaking from the Wall | 3
First Sunday | 4
COMMUNION / UBUNTU / The Lord's Supper | 6
We Come | 8
YHWH: God Feminine and Masculine | 10
Presence of God | 12
God's Love | 13
Our Invitation | 14
Offerings of Joy | 15

Advent
And This Is Love | 19
Pursue JOY! | 20
Hope, Anyhow! | 21
Be Our Peace, O Lord | 23

Christmas and Epiphany | 27
When the Lights Went Out in Bethlehem | 29
Mary's Prayer: What I Knew | 32
Epiphany: Children's Lesson | 35
Baptism of the Lord Ritual | 37

December
World AIDS Day (1) | 41
International Day of Persons with Disabilities (3) | 43
Kwanzaa (26–January 1) | 45
Watchnight, Holy Ground (31-January 1) | 46

Ordinary Time

January
New Years: Awesome Encounters | 53
Martin Luther King Jr. Day (Third Monday) | 54

February
Black History Month | 57
African Heritage Sunday: Hope in Our Heritage | 59
I See Soweto With Christ like Eyes | 61
And Now, I Cannot Go Back | 63
More Than a History, a Lineage, and a Legacy | 65
Black Love Is Always Revolutionary (13) | 67
St. Valentine's Day (14): With Love, God | 69
National African American Read-In: They Can't Ban Our Stories | 71

March
Creation | 75
This Season of Creation | 76

Lent
Ash Wednesday: Remember Our Dust | 81
Palm Sunday Hosanna! | 83
Hosanna! A Red-Carpet Welcome for a King | 84
Maundy Thursday: At the Last Supper | 85
Jesus, the Disabled Empath | 86
Holy Week Heaviness | 90
Good Friday: Midnight Dark at Midday | 91
Holy Saturday Silence: Vigil | 93

April
　Sacred Vessels: A Litany for Black Maternal Health | 97
　Victims of Violent Crimes | 99
　National Crime Victims Week: Lives Lost, Love Reigns | 101
　Mental Health Awareness: On this Side of Heaven | 103
　Washington DC Emancipation (16)
　　"We the People of DC" 2024 | 105

Easter and Eastertide
　Jesus Is . . . Alive! | 109
　Resurrection: Call to Worship | 111
　Raised | 113
　Eastertide: Anticipation | 115
　Ascension Day | 116

Pentecost
　21st Century Upper Room Experience | 121
　Pentecost: Suddenly! | 122
　Trinity Sunday (Sunday after Pentecost) | 123

May
　Mental Health Awareness Month | 127
　Mothers Like . . . Me! | 128
　When Mama Was God | 130
　TRANSparent | 133
　Daughters of Zelophehad Must Have Been Womanists | 135
　Women's Day: In the Beginning–God is a Woman! | 136
　Women Honoring God in Word and Deed | 138
　Self-Rising Dough–Celebrating the Past
　　and Living the Future | 139
　African Liberation Day (25) | 142
　Armed Forces Day | 144
　Memorial Day | 147

Ordinary Time

June
African American Music Appreciation Month | 155
"We All, Everyone, Everywhere" Bernice Johnson
    Reagon / LGBTQI+ Solidarity | 158
March on Washington | 160
Gun Violence Awareness | 162
LGBTQI+ Solidarity | 163
LGBT+ Solidarity | 164
LGBTQ+ / BLACK PRIDE: Litany of Celebration
    "Out on the Hill" | 165
Pastoral Installation: Litany of Celebration | 167
Fathers' Day: Our Father, On Earth as He is in Heaven | 169
Gun Violence (7) | 171
Juneteenth (19) | 174

July
Independence Day: What Freedom? | 179
Disabled Pride | 181

August
Seasons Change: What Do You Need Most? | 187
Faith / Yes! | 188

September
National Black Family Reunion Month | 191
Family Reunion: Roll Call | 193
National HBCU Week | 195
Deaf Awareness Week | 198

October
Breast Cancer Awareness: Quiet Killer, Silent Pain | 203
Domestic Violence Month | 205
Diversity, Equity, Inclusion, & Belonging | 208
National Coming Out / Welcome In Day (11) | 211
Stewardship: "Be the Miracle" Capital Campaign | 213
COVID-19: Requiem | 215

November
All Saints Day (1) | 219
Veterans Day (11) | 222
Black Adoption (18) | 223
Transgender Day of Remembrance (20) | 225
Adoption! God's Family Plan | 227
Thanksgiving: "God Gives Godself" | 229
Thanksgiving for Africans in America
   (nee African-Americans) | 232

Pastoral Prayers for the People
Praying People | 237
Asafetida (Acifidity) Bags and Prayer Cloths | 238
Solidarity Sunday: Call for Permanent Cease-Fire | 240
In Expectation: Waiting for a Pastor | 242
God Almighty in Battle for Us | 244
Intercession for the Nations | 245
Kin in Christ | 247
We Come in Confidence | 249
Womanist Travels to Salvador, Bahia, and Accra, Ghana | 252
Prayer for Mother in Distress at Childbirth | 253
Clergywomen Prayer | 254
We Lay Down Our Burdens | 256
Walking with God | 259
The Holy of Holies | 261

Benedictions
Womanist Benediction | 265
Dance in Advance | 267
The Last Time I Preached | 269

Index | 271

Acknowledgments

I love church people, Black church culture, and radically inclusive worship experiences.

I am grateful for the Black church and community that taught me how to code-switch and welcome, to show hospitality and audacity.

I am grateful to my pastor, William A. Young, IV–the first pastor who understood how my passion for words in preaching and poetry was for congregational call-and-response concerts.

I love, love, love the Covenant Baptist United Church of Christ family for embracing my predilection for purple, preaching, and parables.

I am indebted to womanist scholarship for erecting the theological framework to undo rules and make guides to make sense of the word of liberation.

I am grateful for the philosophical acumen and keen eye of my editor, Rev. Babydoll Kennedy.

I admire seminarians at Wesley Theological Seminary who trusted my editorial hand and radically inclusive faith as they developed their catalogs of *Writing for Ministry*.

I appreciate my daughter, who has encouraged me to publish books for two-thirds of her life.

I give God thanks and praise for giving me more words than my stutter or introversion utters.

Preface

Dear Worship Leader or Lay Reader,

In *Hear the Spirit: ritual poetry & radical litanies*, I offer sacred language that bridges ancient truths with our present yearnings. As a womanist preacher, religious studies professor, and performance poet, I have witnessed how traditional liturgy often falls short of embracing our communities' full humanity—particularly for those whose voices have been historically silenced or marginalized.

These culturally competent calls to worship, litanies, poems, and prayers emerge from the intersection of Black church traditions, womanist theology, and liberation spirituality. They speak to both the rhythms of the Christian calendar and the urgent cries of our times—from Advent to Juneteenth, from Pride celebrations to mental health awareness, from personal healing to collective liberation.

Each piece is crafted to create sacred space where all God's children can bring their full selves—African American heritage, LGBTQI+ identities, lived experiences of struggle and triumph, and hopes for transformation. This collection aims not merely to supplement traditional liturgy but to radically reimagine how we gather, pray, and move together toward justice.

Consider these offerings as seeds. Plant them in your particular soil, nurture them with your community's wisdom, and let them bloom in ways that speak truth to your context. May they help us craft worship experiences that honor both our ancestors' faith and our children's futures.

In the Spirit of Love and Liberation,
Rev. Dr. Raedorah C. Stewart

Invocations

Speaking from the Wall

Every time I open my mouth
I'm speaking from the wall
So,
Listen to me now
but hear the Spirit.

First Sunday

Bless the Lord, O my soul, and all that is within me.
Bless God's holy name
Bless the Lord, oh my soul—Let all that we are praise the LORD;
may we never forget the good things God does for us.

First Sunday Tradition—the Lord's Table—Communion
More than a routine ritual.
May we never forget our salvation is a good thing God does for us.

Through the watchful eyes of doorkeepers serving in the front office and in the sanctuary
We praise Your Holy name
In choreographies of technology and dance
We praise Your Holy name
Deacons who care for the congregation and
the trustees who serve with integrity
We praise Your Holy name
With the voices in key, on the drums, and with the strings
We praise Your Holy name
From the pew to the pulpit, in the song, and in the sermon
We praise Your holy name

We bless You, Lord, with everything within us.
We praise Your holy name!

Holy Spirit, sanctify this service to the end that God is glorified, Jesus is on our minds, and Your people are revived.

COMMUNION / UBUNTU / *The Lord's Supper*

As we prepare throughout this service to partake of the Lord's table, let us come with a spirit of humility, repentance, and thanksgiving.

Compassionate God, have mercy on us, we pray.

Let us examine our thoughts, our actions, our motives, and our attitudes toward others.

O Holy God, have mercy and forgive us for our shortcomings.

Help us to remember our responsibility to our families and our neighbors, our stewardship to You, and the work You have given to our hands. Guide us. Awaken us. Energize us for the massive tasks that lie ahead.

O Living God, we stand in need of Your grace, strength, and mercy.

As we eat of the bread, which represents Your body, which is the True and Living Bread, open our eyes to recognize the intimacy that You yearn to share with us.

O Loving God, teach us to love You above all else, even above our ambitions.

As we drink the cup, which represents Christ's blood shed for us, we thank You for the new covenant, "Love ye one another," which is written on our hearts. Help us to live it out. Let us rejoice because our names are written in the book only You can open and close.

Tender Father and Mother, may Your great sacrifice of redeeming love renew us for loving service and for sacrifice for others. Let us worship here and leave refreshed to serve.

Let us not take of this bread and wine if we do not intend to serve others.

May this Lord's Supper energize every area of our lives and enable us to transcend our circumstances, our inadequacies, and our enemies.

God who sees us fully, touches and empowers us so that our lives will be remarkable testimonies of Your presence.

We praise You, O God, who made us Your people through the death and resurrection of Your Son, our Lord.

Abide in us, and throughout this service, our Savior and Redeemer. Fill us with the life-giving power of the Holy Spirit, so that when we leave this place, we will be forever changed. Amen.

We Come

Oh Lord Our God, Creator of Heaven and Earth,
Of all that grows and blooms, of all that is born and breathes–
How marvelous, how majestic, how mysterious is Your Name.
We have signed on, shown up, and are on our way
to the House of the Lord to worship You.

We come rejoicing and weeping.
We come with the quickness of youth
and the slow gait of aged wisdom.
We come out of habit *and*
full of hope in Your new mercies and steadfast love!

We come, in Your Names, every tribe and tongue from
YHWH to ALLAH, The Great Spirit and The Great Mother,
Theos and Jah, Dios, and Oledumare,
Wankan Tanka and Nyame
We come in Your Names, every tribe and every tongue!

We set this service at Your feet
to bring You glory, honor, and praise.
To You and You alone,
We *tehillah*, songs of praise
We *todah*, with arms raised and hand wave

We *kara*, in the dance, toe tap, and sway
We *shabbach*, the hallelujah.
We *shabbach*, the glory
We *shabbach*, theAsé, and the Amen.

So, we welcome You, an audience of One–be glorified today!
We *shabbach* You, Lord.
Asé. Amen.

YHWH: God Feminine and Masculine

Yahweh: God feminine and masculine
Ruah: God feminine
Creator: in whose image the human is made
> We gather to worship You today in the spirit of holiness, under the banner of joy, all because You are worthy!
>
> **You are welcome in this place, tangible and virtual, as we set before You our celebration of who You are to us embodied in womaness.**
>
> We recall Your blessing over us: Did I conceive all this people? Did I give birth to them, that You should say to me, "Carry them in your bosom, as a nurse carries a sucking child, to the land that You promised on oath to their ancestors"? (Num 11:12 NRSV)

For life through You and in You, thank You.
> Accept our offerings now, baptized in the fire of the Holy Ghost.
>
> **Ignite our embers of song that some might be saved.**
>
> Ignite our embers of dance that others might be healed.
>
> **Ignite our embers of testimony to encourage.**
>
> Ignite the embers of the preached Word that hearers would hasten to obey.
>
> **Ignite the embers of every yeah, Asé, and Amen to witness to the world a hope that defies circumstance.**

Yahweh: God feminine and masculine
Ruah: God feminine
Creator: in whose image the human is made
You are welcome here.

Presence of God

God who created–we who believe, those who doubt,
and those who don't–WE sing songs of joy from our hearts,
declare Your praise on our tongues,
and utterly depend on You with prayers on our lips!

Our presence in Your presence is resistance
to all foes of our culture, class, and conditions.
Our songs of ascent demonstrate audacious faith
in Your embodied promises and embodied power
in which we live, and move, and have our being.

As an audience of One God of many names, welcome.
Holy Spirit, sanctify our assembling. In the name of Jesus.
Asé. Amen.

God's Love

Sometimes our actions contradict Your commandments
And our words are inadequate to express our repentance
Yet, You love us just the same, Lord God.
So, we offer every hymn and hand to give You praise.
We lay our lives on the altar as living sacrifices
to show up as servants in the world.
We came to worship, and we pray You are delighted by our pure hearts and pleased with praise from our earthen vessels.
Have Your way Holy Spirit. Have Your way.
For Here we are, in Your presence, and You are welcome here!
Asé. Amen.

Our Invitation

Thank you, God, for accepting our invitation to dwell with us
Thank You for making a tabernacle for us to gather
> **Thank You for the power of the Holy Ghost that compelled us to meet with You and fellowship with one another this morning.**

Now, into Your hands, we put our praise on string instruments, percussion, wind instruments, and tambourine.
> **Into Your hands, we place our prayers of invocation, supplication, and intercession.**

Into Your hand, we steward our time, talent, and treasures
> **Lord, place this preacher under Your hand to hear from You, in Your hand to speak for You and keep her hedged in as she represents You in the world, through word, work, and deed.**

Ah, thank you, God, for accepting our invitation to dwell with us.
> **Hallelujah. Asé.**
> **God is Here! Amen!**

Offerings of Joy

Benevolent Lord, we pray that these offerings are given with joy and thanksgiving, reflecting the cheerful spirit You desire from those who love You in word and deed.

Like Your servant David prayed (1 Chronicles 29:14): "But who am I, and who are my people, that we should be able to give as generously as this? Everything comes from You, and we have given You only what comes from Your hand." Indeed, Lord, we acknowledge that we are merely stewards of Your blessings.

So, use these offerings, O God, as You used the five loaves and two fish, multiplying them for Your glory and the advancement of Your kin'dom, to be instruments of Your love, bringing hope to the hopeless, comfort to the afflicted, and the light of Your gospel to those who walk in darkness.

In the name of Jesus, receive our loving obedience and living sacrifice! Asé. Amen

Advent

And This Is Love

Oh, Most High, we sing praises to Your Name: *Messiah, Redeemer, Savior, the Christ!*
    Oh, this is Love!
As children, we were often singing: *God's got the whole world, in God's hand!*
    This is Love!
We grew up reciting: *For God so loved the world, that God gave us the only begotten Son to save us from all sin.*
    And this is Love!
Growing in faith and knowledge, we live under grace knowing that: *Nothing, but nothing, can separate us from the love of God that is in Christ Jesus!*
    This is Love!
And so, we vow this Advent, to keep the commandments: First, to love the Lord our God with our whole hearts, souls, and minds; and second, to love our neighbors and strangers, visible congregants and virtual members, and one another as we love ourselves!
    God is Love. Jesus is Love Incarnate. And in the power of the Holy Spirit, we are Love in Action! Asé and Amen.

Pursue JOY!

In valleys low and mountains high,
When storm clouds gather in the sky,
There dwells a joy that cannot fade—
A gift divine when Jesus came.

This joy runs deeper than our pain,
Beyond life's losses, beyond its gain.
Joy gifts us grace that sets us free,
Ever flowing for eternity.

So lift your hearts, beloved friends,
And pursue joy that never ends.
In Christ alone, our spirits soar,
Until we reach heaven's shore.

Pursue joy until joy arises,
In songs of praise that reach the skies.
Through every storm and gentle rain,
Christ's unspeakable joy shall ever reign.

Pursue JOY!

Hope, Anyhow!

Listen as the Spirit speaks to the Church: "Seek the peace and prosperity of the city to which I have carried you into exile. Pray to the LORD for it, because if it prospers, you too will prosper." (Jer 29:7)

> **Speak, Spirit, speak to the righteous workers of peace, justice, mercy, and love.**

We might want to see white privilege protected by laws that protect their lawlessness, but...

> **We seek life more abundantly, anyhow, when we show up to vote, canvass our community with COVID awareness, and screen films that are anti-everything You love!**

We do not choose for our hearts to break a bit more every time we hear of virulent red blood expelled from innocent Black bodies being the reward of a *Manifesto* of evil being sold to this nation as a "bad day," a "toothache," and "mental illness," but...

> **We seek justice, anyhow, by relentlessly defending truth instead of the "American way."**

We wish that affordable housing was not politicized as the likely deciding factor in the District's mayoral race when escalating homelessness is evident under every overpass in makeshift "tent cities," but...

> **We extend mercy, anyhow, when we protest by pen, on the phone, and in person to advocate for a more humane response to this misfortuned human reality.**

We want a nation where women, and only women, have agency over their bodies; where trans people are not unduly taxed for adequate health care; and where food deserts and contaminated ecology are not a blight on our social landscape, but...

> **We are not apathetic, not at all, about fighting against health care disparities, baby formula genocide, and industrial desecration of the Earth.**

But, we hope, anyhow, for peace and prosperity when we pray to You for the times and seasons, wards and districts, nations and cities, where we live today!

> **Yes, we hope, anyhow, for peace and prosperity that we may not see in our lifetime but is nonetheless pleasing to our ancestors and a legacy to generations to come.**

All: We did not choose this exile, but WE are the righteous remnant who dare to hope in God's love–anyhow! *Hallelujah! Asé! Amen!*

Be Our Peace, O Lord

In a world fractured by division and discord,
Be our peace, O Lord.

When nations rage and borders become battlegrounds,
Be our peace, O Lord.

In regions torn by war, where children fear and families flee,
Be our peace, O Lord.

When political debates turn neighbors into enemies and immigrants into criminals,
Be our peace, O Lord.

In the face of natural disasters that leave communities broken and hearts heavy,
Be our peace, O Lord.

When fear of the future scarcity drives us to distrust one another,
Be our peace, O Lord.

When economic uncertainty causes anxiety and sleepless nights,
Be our peace, O Lord.

In our cities where gunfire echoes and violence breeds more violence,
Be our peace, O Lord.

When social media amplifies anger and drowns out understanding,
Be our peace, O Lord.

In our churches, where differences in doctrine sometimes overshadow our unity in Christ,
Be our peace, O Lord.

In our homes, where unspoken words and hidden hurts create walls between loved ones,
Be our peace, O Lord.

When our hearts are troubled and our spirits restless,
Be our peace, O Lord.

Prince of Peace,
You who calmed the storms and reconciled heaven to earth,
Walk with us through the chaos of our time.
Make us instruments of Your peace—

Where there is hatred, let us sow love;
Where there is injury, pardon;
Where there is doubt, faith;
Where there is despair, hope;
Where there is darkness, light;
Where there is sadness, joy.

Not by our might, but by Your Spirit,
Not for our glory, but for Your kingdom,

Make us channels of Your peace in our time.
Asé. Amen.

Christmas and Epiphany

When the Lights Went Out in Bethlehem

Again this year at Christmas time
There are no lights in Bethlehem
And with the temporary cease-fire
There are even no bombs in the night sky

In the land of broken dreams and falling skies,
Forty-four thousand stories silenced, forty-four thousand cries
A report unfolds, stark and unafraid
Of the devastation mercilessly made

Nations speak with a voice of thunder
Of displacement, of families torn asunder
Ninety percent of Palestinians were driven from their home
Forced to wander, forced to roam

Zionist rhetoric studied, one hundred deep
Revealing words that make nations weep
Dehumanization etched in official speech
A sorrow beyond what language can reach

Generations wiped out in a single breath
Entire families consumed by unrelenting death
Children's shoes left standing alone
Their futures scattered in dust and stone

"Genocide," they declare with trembling might
A calculated erasure, hidden from light
No safe place, no mercy's embrace
Just rubble and pain across this fractured space

Fourteen months ago, Hamas attacked
Out armed as always, Israel struck back
But beyond the rhetoric, beyond the blame
Lies a human cost too great to name

World leaders stand firm, and the message clear:
"Genocide must stop now, this must end here"
A wake-up call to America that turns away
Enabling the suffering that continues day by day

In the margins of history, in the spaces between breaths
A people's existence hangs by threads
A poem of pain, a testament true
To the human cost of an unending rue

Again, this year at Christmas time
There are no lights in Bethlehem
And with the temporary cease-fire
There are even no bombs in the night sky

Still, we legislate, protest, and pray
That a permanent cease-fire rules the day
To lay claim to a plot of land for a few
Is not the hope of the Torah Jew

And so with them, we choose to stand
Desiring for peace throughout the land
Where Jesus was born, the Messiah came
We long for a lighted Christmas in Bethlehem.

Mary's Prayer: What I Knew

Lord of all creation,
You who chose me, humble daughter of Israel,
How do I answer when they ask, *"Did you know?"*

Did I know?
I knew the weight of angel wings
In the air that morning, heavy with glory.
I knew fear that made my knees weak,
And courage that came like dawn—unexpected, unstoppable.
I knew what it meant to say "yes" without understanding all.

Did I know?
I knew the flutter of divine life beneath my heart,
The stirring of eternity in my womb.
I knew Elizabeth's joy, the leap of John,
The prophecies tumbled from her lips like living water.
I knew my song would echo through generations.

Did I know?
I knew the pain of birthing God,
The holy terror of holding infinity in my arms.
I knew shepherds' wonder and Magi's gifts,

Simeon's prophecy pierced like a sword,
The midnight flight to Egypt, my child pressed close to my breast.

Did I know He would heal the sick?
> *I saw compassion in His infant's eyes.*

Did I know He would calm the storms?
> *I heard His first cry command creation's awe.*

Did I know He would raise the dead?
> *I held Life who wore my flesh.*

Did I know?
I knew fragments and glimpses,
Like stars scattered across the night's darkness.
I knew questions that burned like incense,
Treasured each mystery in my heart,
Pondered them in the quiet hours before dawn.

But did I know He would hang upon a cross?
> *I knew Simeon's sword would pierce my soul.*

Did I know death would bow before Him?
> *I knew no grave could hold the Morning Star.*

Did I know He would save our souls?
> *I knew what Gabriel promised: He would save His people from their sins.*

O Lord, I knew enough to trust,
Enough to follow, enough to believe.
I knew enough to stand beneath His cross,
To watch Love pour out in water and blood,
To wait through Sabbath's silence,
To receive Him back, risen, glorious, triumphant.

"Did I know?"
I knew what every mother knows:
That love costs everything and is worth it all,
That every child is a mystery and a miracle,
That saying "yes" to You means walking by faith
When sight fails and questions linger.

And now I know, as then I trusted,
That Your plan unfolds like a flower in darkness,
Perfect, beautiful, beyond imagining.
I only hope that those who ask, *"Did you know?"*
Learn to trust as I did,
One step, one day, one prayer at a time,
Until faith becomes sight
And all shall know as they are fully known.

In the name of my baby and God's Son,
Asé. Amen.

Epiphany: Children's Lesson

Sometimes when you're solving math at school,
Or trying to remember a tricky rule,
The answer pops into your mind so clearly,
And all the puzzle pieces just appear!
    That's an epiphany, oh-oh-oh!
    When something clicks and now you know!

Epiphany is a special Christian holiday that happens on January 6th, twelve days after Christmas. Some people call it "Three Kings Day" and that funny song "The Twelve Days of Christmas" can help you remember the importance of Epiphany to us. Let me tell you the wonderful story behind it!

Remember the Christmas story, with baby Jesus in the manger? Well, Epiphany celebrates when Three Kings (sometimes called Magi or Wise Men) finally found baby Jesus by following a bright star in the night sky. They had traveled a very long way from their homes bringing special gifts to the new baby, Jesus!:

- One brought gold because Jesus was a king
- One brought frankincense, a sweet-smelling candle used in worship
- One brought myrrh, a very rare, expensive perfume

You may be thinking, "What odd gifts to bring to a baby shower!" when most babies need diapers, formula, and a lot more diapers! However more important than the gifts were that three people from different countries came together to worship baby Jesus. By doing so they taught us that Jesus came for everybody from every culture, not just one group of people!

Now, that's an epiphany, yes, it's true,
When understanding breaks right through!

Did you know that people all over the world celebrate Epiphany in fun ways? Even though folk are still excited over Christmas gifts, some families exchange gifts on Epiphany, too. In some countries, children leave their shoes out the night before, hoping to find treats inside in the morning. A lot of people enjoy special foods like "King Cake," a round cake with a tiny baby Jesus doll hidden inside. Everybody gets excited to see who finds the toy baby Jesus in their slice of cake! And some communities have parades with people dressed as the Three Kings leading the way!

For Christians, we celebrate this day when we understand that Jesus was very special–he was actually God's Son who came to live on Earth.

Stars and gifts and toy babies in cake, are odd things to see
But they tell the story of Jesus–that's what we call an epiphany!

[Dismiss children to Children's Church with a small gift and have cupcakes waiting for them!]

Baptism of the Lord Ritual

Altar: *Designate four congregants to bring these items to the altar*

- Bowl of water with blue, smooth stones in the bottom
- White candle and wand lighter
- Dove figurine, picture, or art
- Bible (a paraphrased version tells a simple story)

Prayer
Minister: God our Creator, today we remember Jesus' baptism in the Jordan River and our baptisms in fancy pools, galvanized tanks, or shallow lakes and streams. Through water and Your Holy Spirit, You claim us as Your beloved children. Help us remember and celebrate this special gift. Amen.

Scripture Reading
Deacon: Matthew 3:13–17 (The Baptism of Jesus)

Water Ritual
Minister: In baptism, God washes us clean and welcomes us into the family of God. Let us remember our baptisms.

Each person comes forward one at a time. Invite them to:

- Say the date (or year) of their baptism

- Take a smooth stone from the bowl of water

After each person retrieves a stone:
Minister: You are God's beloved child!

Candle Lighting
Deacon: Lights candle

Minister: This light reminds us that in baptism, we receive Christ's light. We are called to share this light with others.

All: With God's help, we commit to shining God's light in the world!

Blessing
Minister: May God, who has begun a good work in you through baptism, continue to bless you with peace, joy, and love. Remember that you are God's beloved child today and always.

All: Asé. Amen.

DECEMBER

World AIDS Day (1)

Merciful God, on this World AIDS Day, we come to You with hearts full of compassion and hope. We pray:

For Your beloved children living with HIV and AIDS:
> Grant them strength for each day, access to the care and medicine they need, and freedom from stigma and fear. Surround them with Your love and the support of caring communities.

For we who have lost loved ones to AIDS:
> Hold us in our grief, keep their precious memories alive, and help us honor their legacy by working for a world free of AIDS.

For healthcare workers and researchers:
> Guide their hands and minds as they provide care and seek new treatments. Give them wisdom, persistence, and compassion in this healing work.

For advocates and educators:
> Strengthen our voices as we fight discrimination, spread understanding instead of fear, and teach ways to prevent HIV transmission. Help us build bridges of compassion and understanding.

For those who face barriers to care:

Open doors of access to treatment, break down walls of prejudice and discrimination and move hearts to respond with justice and kindness.

For our young people:
Grant them knowledge to protect themselves, wisdom to make healthy choices, and hearts of compassion for those affected by HIV/AIDS.

Move us all to action:
To support our siblings living with HIV and AIDS, to remember those we have lost, to educate ourselves and others, and to work for the day when AIDS is no more.

We pray for wholeness, healing, understanding, and hope. May we be Your hands of comfort, Your voice of justice, and Your heart of love in our world.

Asé. Amen.

International Day of Persons with Disabilities (3)

Creator God, who formed each person in Your divine image,
We celebrate Your creative love in every life.

For those who roll rather than walk, we see God's image moving among us.
For those who speak with their hands, we see God's image communicating grace.

For those who read with their fingers, we see God's image touching our world.
For those who see the world dimly, we see God's image offering new vision.

For those who are neurodivergent, we see God's image teaching us wisdom.
For those who need support for daily tasks, we see God's image in helping.

For those who use assistive devices, we see God's image speaking through technology.
For those who experience life intensely, we see God's image awakening awareness.

For those who face barriers in our communities,
We commit to removing obstacles and building ramps.

For those whose gifts are often overlooked,
We commit to recognizing and including them in leadership.

For those who have been excluded,
We commit to creating spaces of true belonging.

In our diverse bodies, God's image shines.
In our diverse minds, God's image thinks.

In our diverse ways of being, God's image lives.
In our shared community, we are all God's beloved children.

Holy One, help us to see Your face in each person we meet, build community where every person's dignity is honored, every person's gifts are celebrated, and every person's presence reveals Your image. Make us one body with many members, united in Your love. Asé. Amen.

Kwanzaa (26–January 1)

Imani! We Declare Faith in God, Family, and Community

Affirming our African heritage of being made in the image of Our Creator, we declare our Faith in God, the Alpha and the Omega, the One in whom time is marked by *kairos* (καιρός) and unlimited by *chronos* (χρόνος). Habari Gani!

> **Imani! We declare faith in God, who makes all things beautiful at the appointed time.**

Habari Gani!

> **Imani! We declare faith in family: those we are born into, those chosen and who chose us, those found by Your faithfulness to set the lonely in families.**

Habari Gani!

> **Imani! We declare faith in community defined by universal humanity, described by zip codes and quadrants, made through the wonder of Wi-Fi, the internet, and social media!**

Faith brings us together in worship and works that we become Beloved Community. Together we hope for happiness to abound for You, and You, and all around!

Joyous Kwanzaa **and** ***Happy New Year*** **from our family of faith to yours. Asé! Amen!**

Watchnight, Holy Ground (31-January 1)

Before worship: play recordings of Negro Spirituals as people enter. Ministers and Church Leaders process into African drumming.

Call to Worship
We gather as our ancestors gathered
Waiting, watching, hoping, praying

We gather as they gathered on Freedom's Eve
Standing between bondage and liberty, darkness and light

We gather in the spirit of their faith believing that trouble doesn't last always.

On this holy ground, we remember. On this holy ground, we give thanks. On this holy ground, we look forward with hope.

Remembering

Layperson: Share the story of Watchnight 1862 and its significance

Congregational Hymn: "Guide My Feet While I Run This Race"

Testimonies of the Elders: Invite them to share memories of Watchnight services from the past

Libations

Minister: Pour water from a pitcher into a live plant or a bowl
Congregation: calls the names of ancestors by "We remember ... We honor ... We thank ..."

Reflections

For the trials we faced this year ...
Thank You, Lord, You brought us through!

For the losses we grieved ...
Thank You, Lord, You brought us through!

For the victories we celebrated ...
Thank You, Lord, You brought us through!

Songs of the Journey

- "Precious Lord, Take My Hand"
- "We've Come This Far by Faith"

Anticipation

Deacon: Isaiah 43:18–19: "Do not remember the former things ... I am about to do a new thing."

Minister: God of new beginnings, as we enter this new year, thank you for bringing us this far. When we get weary, grant us rest. When we are uncertain, give us courage. When doors open, make us bold. Where there's injustice, help us act. Guide our steps with hope and light our path with grace throughout this coming year.

Soloist: "Hold On Just a Little While Longer"

Sermon: Minister's Choice based on theme for the year or exhortation

Pray Out, Shout In

Minister: invite congregation to kneel, sit, or stand to pray personal prayers

Minister: God who is the Alpha of all times and Omega eternally, we give You praise for bringing us over the chronos of time into Your kairos of purpose! Renew our passion to be Your people of love, joy, hope, and faith!

"How I Got Over"

"Victory is Mine"

Other joyful praise medley

Benediction

Minister: Lord God, we bless Your people to travel from this place in safety and throughout the year in peace. Thank you for calling us to the ministry of unity in community, justice in the nation, peace in our world, and joy for the journey that is this new year. Asé. Amen!

"Walk together, children, don't you get weary . . ."

Ordinary Time

JANUARY

New Years: Awesome Encounters

We have come into the House of the Lord, *again*. May our routine be disrupted with an awesome encounter in the Spirit.

Attune our ears to hear what Spirit says to the Church...

When we sing familiar hymns and spiritual songs. May we encounter new meanings and renewed messages of our faith.

Create in us clean hearts O God, that can be used in Your service...

When we open the doors of the church on Thursdays to feed our neighbors and on Sundays to encounter the family of God.

Open our minds to understand deep wisdom in plain teaching...

When we meet weekly to study biblical precepts for living. May we encounter opportunities to give legs to our learning.

Remind us of Your faithfulness morning by morning...

When we rise to seek Your face and rest in Your grace at night. May each encounter with You lead us to divine awe.

We have come into the House of the Lord, again, expecting another awesome encounter with the Holy One as we worship. Asé and Amen.

Martin Luther King Jr. Day (Third Monday)

Divine Spirit of Justice and Love, we pause to honor Your servant Martin,
> Who dared to dream amid nightmares,
> Who preached love in the face of hatred,
> Who moved forward when terror said, "Stand back."

Thank you for his prophetic vision that still calls us to the mountaintop,
> Still challenges our comfortable silence,
> Still demands we choose beloved community
> Over chaos, courage over complicity.

Grant us the strength to continue his work—
> Not just to quote his words but to live them,
> Not just to celebrate his dream but to build it,

Until justice rolls down like waters,
And freedom rings from every mountaintop.

Asé. Amen.

FEBRUARY

Black History Month

We call upon our ancestors who crossed oceans in chains
Yet kept their spirits free.

We remember the ones who built nations with stolen hands
And created beauty from brutality.

We honor the voices that sang freedom songs in a strange land
Yet made light shine through their melodies.

We celebrate the teachers who wrote wisdom in margins
And turned whispers into declarations.

We praise the marchers who faced dogs and water hoses
Yet transformed fear into fierce love.

We uplift the mothers who planted seeds of revolution in their children
And harvested hope from concrete gardens.

We stand now, carrying their dreams in our DNA and strength through our veins!

We are the answers to their prayers. We are the morning stars they wished upon. We are the freedom dreams they never let die.

Ashe. Amen. Let it be so.

African Heritage Sunday: Hope in Our Heritage

In the beginning, when God created humanity, God created Africans! Africans are brilliant architects of culture, beautiful bodies in tune with deep vibrations of the universe, and Black in all hues of the image and likeness of God our creator.

Africans are communal and connectional, mysterious and metaphysical, strong because we have to be, and joyful because we choose to be.

Africans were enslaved and Africa was plundered. New names were forced upon us, our backs bled from lashes of insidious rage, and mothers wailed for their living babies longer than we mourned over our dead.

Africans, taken in violence, survived being traded in North America, South America, and the Caribbean.

Africans also rebelled in Virginia, revolted in Haiti, and reclaimed our time in Washington, DC.

Africans remember the God of ancient Egypt and the God of the Serengeti as the same God of Ferguson, Baltimore, and Texas.

Africans call on God who is not blind to murdering us with impunity, the injustice of legalizing marijuana after 40 years of incarcerating us for possession for personal use, and inequity in the fallacy of *separate but equal* in schools in the 60s and technology today.

Africans *still* make bricks without straw. Africans *still* follow the drinking gourd. Africans *still* braid liberation

in our hair. Africans *still* pour libations in homage to our ancestors and to the homies who are no longer with us.

In the beginning, when God created humanity, God created Africans! We are not three-fifths human, we are Black and proud. We are not uncivilized, we are the progenitors of civilization. We are not the problem, we are the promise that God's love endures forever, and God's vengeance shall come upon our enemies.

In the beginning, when God created humanity, God created Africans! This truth is our heritage and our hope. Asé and Amen.

I See Soweto With Christ like Eyes

It really was no surprise
To see Soweto through Christ like eyes.

I see the glory of God's Only Son
I see joy and victories won
I see pain of many tears shed
I see the anointing upon your head

I see wives longing to give
I see girls desiring to live
I see women so dressed up and fancy
I see you all in the aisles dancing

I see brothers willed to survive.
I see boys hoping to stay alive
I see men wanting Power the most
I see you all filled with the Holy Ghost

I see your anger in righteousness.
I see you walk in blessedness
I see you praise from sun to sun
I see you pray for the change to come

I see Soweto, coming up from the dust
I see Soweto, in God always trust
I see Soweto, and I'll watch you rise
`Cause I see Soweto, through Christ like eyes.

And Now, I Cannot Go Back

To Moira and the Soweto Women

Picture books and postcards just don't tell your story well
Printed papers and TV. sets chose which lies to tell.

You know, the ones that kill a people of the human race
Who by God's creation first occupied this place.

And now, I cannot go back, having seen You with my own eyes
And now, I cannot go back as thousands of others die.

No, no, I cannot go back—we've even broken bread together
And now I cannot go back without my sister, my brother.

No, I cannot go back across great waters and land
Now I cannot go back to a nation that doesn't understand.

And now I cannot go back to wondering where You are
Now I cannot go back with a distance not so very far.

No, I cannot go back
    Without so much of me still here
I just cannot go back
    Without longing for You near
I cannot go back
    You have a truth worth telling
I cannot go back Silent,
    your story is too compelling.

And now, I cannot go back.
    As though I am whole
No, I cannot go back
    With an unchanged soul
I cannot go back
    Without leaving me behind
I cannot go back
    Without You always on my mind.

More Than a History, a Lineage, and a Legacy

In the beginning, God created more than a history, a lineage, and a legacy–God created our African heritage! Can I get an "Amen!"

Amen! The antecedent to this America's history books is our African ancestors from whom they took...

Africa's earth's yield of diamonds hewn out of God's imagination and beauty of melanated blackness fashioned in God's image. Can I get an "Asé?"

Asé! However–even being ripped from the breast of Mother Africa and transported as stolen goods and spoils of war did not break our soul–okayyy!

I know that's right! And we didn't just survive–we thrived, and we are thriving still.

In God's image, we thrive in the mitochondrial DNA of the Black woman through which all the possible variations for every kind of human being mutate. Can I get an "Asé?"

Asé! Our history as scientists turned peanuts into soap, mayo, and adhesives; and unraveled the mystery of gravity to send humans into space. We thrive!

Asé! Our history of training women as direct sales entrepreneurs of beauty products in the early 1900s was the business model for that other company launched in the mid-1960s. We thrive!

Asé! Our history as inventors reimagined gun-play as super soakers summer-time water fun-play; and patented the folding chair iconized in the Alabama waterfront liberation brawl of 2023. We thrive!

> Asé! Our history as artists includes poets whose eloquence was doubted since we weren't supposed to be able to learn to read, write, and recite in the King's language; and as singers who earned the EGOT (Emmy, Grammy, Oscar, and Tony) awards after being told we don't fit the image of a pop star! We thrive!

Asé! Our history as Constitutional experts defies the colonization of the USA presidential lineage and disrupts legislated gaslighting with "No matter how hard you try, I am not the one on trial here!" We thrive!

> African heritage is enthroned in the heavens and embodied in the Diaspora. From when God made us to how God keeps us, we are God's people, indeed. Asé! Amen!

Black Love Is Always Revolutionary (13)

When we love, galaxies rearrange themselves into new constellations of possibility—
our melanin glowing like starlight against the darkness they tried to use to erase us.

Baby, the way your soul blooms beneath these brown hands
is sweeter than summer's first peach,
defiant as dandelions pushing through concrete,
holy as Big Mama's Sunday prayers.

They never understood how we could laugh so deep it shakes ancestral memory,
how we could kiss so tenderly after centuries tried to harden our hearts,
how we could dance in chains and still teach our children to fly.

But here we are, creating forever in each heartbeat,
building temples with our touched fingertips,
speaking tomorrow into existence with each "I love you"
that escapes our revolutionary mouths.

Black Love is freedom song
is healing balm
is ancient wisdom

is future promise
is proof
that no matter what they stole,
they could never take
the magic of us
loving us
saving us
choosing us
again, and again and again.

Beloved, when I hold you, I hold everything we ever were
and everything we're gonna be—
a love story written in starlight, signed in melanin,
sealed with joy.

St. Valentine's Day (14): "With Love, God"

God is love. God loved us first. God's love is everlasting. God's love is for everyone!

We remember God's love through the Christian martyr St. Valentine after whom St. Valentine's Day is named.

God is love–a love victorious over death, hell, and the grave–by which the world is saved through Christ Jesus.

God's love is costly, yet free to all who believe that there is no greater love.

God loved us first–from the idea of creating the first human to numbering each of our days before we took our first breath.

God's love is creative, showing up through people and preaching, through music and dance, through story and art.

God's love is everlasting–present with Africans thriving in our homeland, present in the hull of hatred during the Middle Passage, present on the auction block...

...present in slave uprisings and civil disobedience, present despite Jim Crow, present through movements for civil rights and Black Lives...

...present in Black bodies, Black brilliance, Black resistance, and Black joy!

God's love is for everyone! To receive flowers and chocolates, or not, God loves You. To dine over candlelight and gifts, or not, God loves You.

God's love is for everyone–a love where differences are celebrated, diversity is honored, and every dividing wall is transformed into a welcome table!

God is love. God loved us first. God's love is everlasting. God's love is for everyone! *Asé and Amen.*

National African American Read-In: They Can't Ban Our Stories

Reading is resistance, knowledge is power,
every banned book makes us stand a little taller

We read-in, we speak-in
We teach-in, we dream-in
Our children deserve to know
Where they come from, where they can go

They're scared of Toni Morrison's tales.
Afraid of Maya's cage that wailed
But we keep reading, keep teaching, keep reaching
Through every page, our spirits are healing

We read-in, we speak-in
We teach-in, we dream-in
Our children deserve to know
Where they come from, where they can go

From Frederick Douglass to bell hooks
We pass down freedom through our books
Each word is a seed of liberation
Growing strong through every generation

We read-in, we speak-in
We teach-in, we dream-in
Our children deserve to know
Where they come from, where they can go

They ban our books because they know
The power of our stories' flow
But we keep reading anyway
In living rooms, in parks, all-day

We read-in, we speak-in
We teach-in, we dream-in
Our children deserve to know
Where they come from, where they can go

Reading is our birthright, knowledge sets us free
Every banned book is a key to liberty

Every banned book helps us rise and BE!
Every banned book helps us rise and BE!
Every banned book helps us rise and BE!
Asé. Amen.

MARCH

Creation

O Lord, grant us the grace to respect and care for Your creation.
   Lord, hear our prayer.
O Lord, bless all of Your creatures as a sign of Your wondrous love.
   Lord, hear our prayer.
O Lord, help us to end the suffering of the poor and bring healing to all of Your creations.
   Lord, hear our prayer.
O Lord, help us to use our technological inventiveness to undo the damage we have done to Your creation and to sustain Your gift of nature.
   Lord, hear our prayer.

This Season of Creation

We are a people called by our Creator to seek justice, love mercy, and walk with God in humility. God knows we are trying. God sees that we are tired.

Summer is not over and we feel the drought of justice as we observe the lead insurrectionist against justice and peace coddled by privilege instead of facing due consequences.

We are a people called by our Creator to imitate love to our neighbors as our Creator has lavished love upon us. God knows we are trying. God sees we are tired.

School has just begun for children in Wards 7–a food desert across the river from gentrified opulence–and way too many of them rely on lunchroom nourishment to feed their yearning minds.

We are a people called by our Creator to speak truth to power against Northeast urban forests becoming graveyards of rusted-out cars and building debris–a sight not seen among the foliage along Rock Creek Park. God knows we are trying. God sees we are tired.

The vitality of African American neighborhoods has been ravished like Africa's diamonds, cobalt, history, and culture by venture capitalists seeking all we have to devour.

But we are yet the people of God, our Creator–the one who gives us strength in youth and witty inventions to make bricks without straw.

In this Season of Creation, we partner with the Creator of heaven and earth, the universe and eternity, and all that dwells therein, to create refreshing streams in the desert.

In this Season of Creation, we partner with our Creator to elect and support leadership after God's own heart–ones who are more hungry for supermarkets and affordable housing than for personal popularity.

In this Season of Creation, we seek environmental justice, love clean air with low emissions, and walk the way of pleasing God who gave us dominion over the Earth.

Our hope for justice is God-promised.

Our light of God's love repels darkness.

Our walk to protest testifies to God's peace.

ALL: God knows we are trying. God gives us strength so that we do not get weary in doing well by all God has created. *Asé! Amen!*

Lent

Ash Wednesday: Remember Our Dust

Holy One, on this day of ashes and remembrance, we come marked with mortality, carrying both our divinity and our dust, our brokenness and our belonging. We confess that we have forgotten the sacred soil from which we spring—earth mixed with Divine breath, stardust stirred with Spirit's power.

In a world that demands our constant doing, we pause to remember our being. In a society that preaches perfection, we embrace our beautiful imperfections. Remember us, O God, in our dust-ness:

> When we forget to rest,
> When we hide our wounds,
> When we deny our need,
> When we reject our limits,
> When we run from our shadows,
> When we turn from our neighbors,
> When we close our hearts to grace.

Mark us again with the truth: that our fragility is not our failing, that our limitations are not our liability, that our dust is holy because You breathe through it, and that our brokenness makes room for Your light.

In this season of turning and returning, may these ashes be more than mortality's reminder—may they be seeds of transformation, planted in the fertile soil of Your mercy.

Asé. Amen.

Palm Sunday Hosanna!

Triumphant Lord, We rejoice in Your entry into the world and into our lives! You entered the rebellious city that later rejected you:
Hosanna!

Joining with the crowds, we sing Your praises and exalt Your reign,
    but even so, our hearts are far from true worship,
    our minds are distant from true understanding.
Hosanna!

Help us to reflect in our lives the glory of Your Son
    and to live faithfully here and now.
Hosanna!

Bring us home again and impart within us a new song of joy and celebration.
Hosanna!
Hosanna!
Hosanna!

Hosanna! A Red-Carpet Welcome for a King

Hosanna!
Blessed is He who comes in the name of the Lord!
We gather to witness the Triumphal Entry of a Messiah sent to overthrow Empire and set the captives free!
Hosanna!
We pave the path of Your approach with fresh palm fronds and metaphorically lay a carpet with the literal 'clothes off our backs!'
Hosanna!
Our makeshift red carpet for the Messiah makes little sense to onlookers but makes plain sense to You of humble means—arriving on a borrowed donkey without the fanfare of stallions, trumpets, and armor.
Hosanna!
The music in the air is our exuberant praise—Blessed is He who comes to fulfill prophecies of old and give us new life!
Hosanna!
With holy expectations handed down by our ancestors of faith, again today, we roll out the red carpet for You, Lord, on this Palm Sunday in our praise and our worship; on the tambourine, skins, and strings; in our prayers and our offerings; in our hand clapping and aisle dancing; in our *Aṣẹ* and *Amen*!
Hosanna!
Blessed is He who comes in the name of the Lord!
Hosanna! Hosanna! Hosanna!

Maundy Thursday: At the Last Supper

- **M** *"Mandatum novum do vobis"* ("a new commandment I give to you"; John 13:34)
- **A** Affirm and welcome your kin, your kind, and all humanity–extending love to the ends of the earth!
- **U** Until I come again, tell others about my faithfulness and sacrifice.
- **N** Nurture is the nature of those who show hospitality in foot-washing, open tables, and greeters at the door.
- **D** Desire fellowship with other believers and encourage one another in psalms, hymns, and spiritual songs.
- **Y** You may be somber on this evening, but hope in this, *"These things I have spoken to you, that my joy may be in you, and that your joy may be full."* (John 15:11)

Jesus, the Disabled Empath

> *"Seeing then that we have a great High Priest who has passed into the Heavens, Jesus the Son of God, let us hold fast to our profession. For we do not have a High Priest who cannot be touched with the feelings of our infirmities, but was in all points tempted as we are, yet without sin. Let us therefore come boldly unto the throne of grace, that we may obtain mercy and find grace to help in time of need."*
> Hebrews 4:14–16 (21st Century King James Version)

Story

I am an empath. Even prior to learning the language of the empath and the even more detailed six types of the empath, I now realize that I was an empath from childhood. I am such an empath, that my sensibilities and sensitivities traverse between that of the emotional empath, physical/medical empath, and intuitive empath. (The other three major empath types to which I do not readily identify are the geomantic empath, plant empath, and animal empath.)

For instance, as young as in kindergarten I befriended "the girl who walked funny" because she wore metal braces and used odd looking crutches. Always tall for my age, I remember telling her to hang on to my back instead of use her crutches when we went to lunch and recess. I don't remember her name, but the sound of her metal braces and crutches are sacred memories; and I recall the odd way we walked in sync as she hugged my waist from behind. I never knew, or cared, why she wore braces, I just knew that I could help her be more normal standing in line and walking to the swings. When we returned after Summer break to first grade, she was no longer at our school. Still, this lingers decades later as a defining moment in my life as a helper—a primary characteristic of an empath.

Fast forward many years ahead helping others in various ways, I was appointed to be the Pastor of Prayer Ministries at a megachurch. What a perfect job for an emotional/intuitive empath! In that role, I found myself prayerfully bearing the burdens of others in a spiritual way like I had carried the body of my young friend in braces. I never knew what person would come to the altar or which prayer request would come across my desk, still, I seemed to have the right words—not just trite scripture quoting—to speak comfort, clarity, and care. Sometimes, we were close enough for me to touch them as we prayed; other times, a lengthy phone call or hand-written prayer sufficed. Most often we shed tears and shared boxes of tissue. I was clear that I was called to this ministry at which being an empath proved to be a good vessel through which the Holy Spirit could comfort others. However, regardless of my awareness of being an empath, my type fails in comparison to the Divine Empath, Jesus Our High-Priest!

Scripture

How often have we heard that Jesus was fully human and fully divine? This apologetic is usually recited when trying to explain that when Jesus wept, slept, got angry, and made wine for a party, that these human experiences were not anthropomorphic. Instead, Jesus was living a fully human experience with a definite divine calling. As he agonized on the Cross, Jesus' last cries sounded very much like our human prayers of concern, distress, and plea. Now, Jesus' disabled body would be the last image of him the crowd of onlookers saw that day. The Most Divine Empath assumed our physical disabilities and spiritual infirmities. Jesus' broken body was the holy sacrifice that made all who believed one with him.

Our High Priest, unlike other cultural deities, is not formed by hand out of matter or imagined by sages. These could not physiologically know the human experience of broken relationship or broken body. But, Our High Priest, who was at the beginning before the beginning began intimately knew the limits of bodily suffering and disabled anguish. Jesus was in touch with what touched us! That is the good news! Therefore, when we gaze upon the cross, amidst some valid albeit competing narratives, might we see Jesus' disabled body as essential to a community called to grace, mercy, and justice?

The word to able-bodied persons would be to not sin by looking away from the visual anguish and inconveniences of the disabled body just as Jesus did not abandon us in the Garden of Gethsemane, on the Via Dolorosa, or from the Cross at noontime. Yes, yes, the temptation to simply take care of disabled persons may seem to be benevolence; however, reconsider that the disabled person is sent to care for you with reciprocity. The temptation to find the loophole in the law to not make churches and public buildings radically inclusive may be cost efficient; however, reconsider that keeping disabled persons out of buildings is a way of keeping us out of sight and out of mind. These are not choices Jesus would make. These are not the choices Jesus made with his broken body on display. Our High Priest, even while disabled, showed aptitude for carrying out his calling and fulfilling his purpose.

The word to disabled persons is that Jesus knows when social systems fail us. Jesus knows when medical treatment is withheld. Jesus knows the agony of pain and the longing for deliverance. Jesus knows abject loneliness, public scrutiny, and openly displayed humiliation. Still, Jesus did not lose focus that he was not his mangled, maligned, and disabled body—he knew he came to the world that the world might be saved! The disabled body is part of the message of salvation. It was this Disabled Body upon which full inclusion into a restored relationship between humanity and God was established. It was through this disabled body that grace came to a mother, mercy to a repentant thief, and justice for us all. Even while tempted to look away from the Cross, hold your gaze upon the disabled body of Jesus the Divine Empath and see yourself as an agent of the message of salvation.

Together then, let us learn from Jesus the Divine Empath to show mercy and to be grace one to another regardless of how our bodies are framed.

Summary

Sure, disabled people move too slow, need too much, and get in the way. Disabled people also afford others a pace to be more present, create ways to improve the quality of life, and are children of God. What you see in those within reach reflects how you ultimately view the sacrifice of the Divine Disabled Empath. You will either look for the grace in us or risk losing the mercy this is to be found to include us in the life of the church and accessibility in culture.

SELAH

Jesus our Savior and Brother models for us the ultimate life of the Empath. For carrying our burdens of separation and exclusion, we have come to know that carrying the burdens of accessibility and inclusion is holy work. May we hear rebuke of the church espousing community without disabled persons in full communion and may we become the empath church that radically includes disabled persons in the next chapters of our church's story. Amen.

Holy Week Heaviness

Merciful God, as we enter Holy Week, turn our hearts again to Jerusalem to the life, death, and resurrection of Jesus Christ. Stir up within us the gift of faith that we may not only praise him with our lips but may follow him in the way of the cross.

The Lord brings light to those in darkness, forgiveness to those who truly confess, and pardon to all who seek to follow Jesus. Rejoice that the steadfast love of the Lord endures forever and ever. In the name of Jesus the Christ, receive the love that never dies and never fails. Asé. Amen.

Good Friday: Midnight Dark at Midday

In reverence, we gather at the foot of the Cross;
Wondering how it is midnight dark in the middle of the day.
   At Calvary, on Golgatha's hill, that mound of misery, and the crucible of the Christ;
We await death that is sure to come at midnight dark in the middle of the day.
   The throng of blood-thirsty spectators has dwindled to fretful whispers of a few women, a lone disciple, and guards of the gruesome inhumanity of a crucifixion.
Perhaps midnight dark in the middle of the day was grace so we could not see the depth of agony on His face.
   But we had a glimmer of hope when Jesus spoke;
Piercing the midnight dark in the middle of the day.
   Each time He spoke we hoped He would unimpale himself;
That would certainly reset the sundial from midnight dark in the middle of the day!
   And Jesus spoke: On behalf of his executioners, *forgive my enemies and the ones just doing their jobs.* **To the guilty one seeking grace,** *because you believe in Me, you will join me eternally.* **And to those who faithfully loved Him,** *take care of one another.*
It was just like Jesus to be carrying on caring for others in the midnight dark in the middle of the day!

And Jesus spoke to His Father this time: *have You forgotten about Me? Is there relief on this tree? Haven't I reached my destiny?*

Were you there, as we eavesdropped on this heavenly exchange while it was midnight dark in the middle of the day?

And, one last time, with His last breath, Jesus spoke and transferred His residency from earth to heaven.

In reverence, again, we gather at the foot of the Cross, still amazed 19 centuries later that it turned midnight dark in the middle of the day.

We do this, to remember You. Asé. Amen.

Holy Saturday Silence: Vigil

In this holy silence, we wait and watch
Through death's deep valley, we hold and hope
Between the cross and empty tomb, we breathe and believe

(Make copies of this prayer to distribute to people after Good Friday service. Encourage them to repeat it softly, slowly, allowing silence between repetitions, each time letting the words settle deeper into the spirit.)

APRIL

Sacred Vessels: A Litany for Black Maternal Health

For Black mothers, sacred vessels of life we raise our voices, demanding justice

For every Black woman who has died bringing life into this world
We say her name, we honor her memory, we demand change.

For the doctors who dismiss our pain
Open their eyes, transform their hearts, make them see our humanity.

For the mothers who advocate from hospital beds
Give them strength, amplify their voices, protect their lives.

For the doulas and midwives carrying ancestral wisdom
Bless their hands, strengthen their spirits, multiply their presence.

For the grandmothers who've taught us to fight
We carry their knowledge, we continue their struggle.

For our babies, born and unborn
We dream of a world where Black birth is safe and celebrated.

For the statistics that haunt us
We are not numbers. We are sacred. We are worthy. We deserve care.

For the systems that fail us
We work to dismantle, to rebuild, to heal.

For our communities to rise up
We organize, we educate, we support each other.

We declare that Black mothers matter, that our lives are precious.
That our babies deserve to know their mothers,
That our communities deserve to thrive.

That our births deserve to be blessed, that our bodies deserve to be honored.
That our pain deserves to be heard, that our joy deserves to be witnessed.

We stand together. We birth justice together. We heal together. We live together
Asé. Amen. Let it be so.

Victims of Violent Crimes

"Hear my cry, O God; attend unto my prayer." (Psalm 61:1)
For those whose lives were stolen in moments of darkness

We remember O Lord, and cry out for justice.

"He will wipe every tear from their eyes. There will be no more death or mourning or crying or pain." (Revelation 21:4)
For the children who never came home

We mourn their lost light and cherish their memory.

"The Lord is near to the brokenhearted and saves the crushed in spirit." (Psalm 34:18)
For the families who carry grief beyond measure

Grant them strength and peace beyond understanding.

"God heals the brokenhearted and binds up their wounds." (Psalm 147:3)
For communities shattered by violence

Heal our wounds and unite us in love.

"Yea, though I walk through the valley of the shadow of death, I will fear no evil: for thou art with me." (Psalm 23:4)
For those who died alone in fear

Hold them in Your eternal embrace.

"Give justice to the weak and the fatherless; maintain the right of the afflicted and the destitute." (Psalm 82:3)
For the voices silenced too soon

Let their stories be heard and remembered.

"Peace I leave with you; my peace I give to You. Not as the world gives do I give to You. Let not your hearts be troubled, neither let them be afraid." (John 14:27)
For all victims of violence, known and unknown

May they find rest in Your perfect peace.

Merciful God, receive the souls of those taken by violence into Your eternal kingdom. Comfort those who mourn, strengthen those who seek justice, and guide us toward a world where such suffering is no more. Grant us the wisdom and courage to stand against violence in all its forms, and to protect the vulnerable among us. Asé. Amen.

National Crime Victims Week: Lives Lost, Love Reigns

She Who Birthed the Earth, our tears water faith in the never-ending cycle of crimes making victims of Your beloved and created.

Weekly, lives are lost to violent crimes: murder and manslaughter, rape, robbery, and aggravated assault. We mourn, yet, we remember those we love with acts of service instead of revenge.

She Who Hears, mothers wail openly like Rizpah, and fathers groan towards the deep when our children have grave markers before having marriages or need therapy by high school.

From 1989 to 1992, the Nation's capital was cited as the Murder Capital of America. So many young lives were lost during this time.

She Who is Strength, this month, 33 years later, we say the names of loved ones in this number and comfort those whose families know the magnitude of this loss even today.

We are just in the fourth month of 2022, and the FBI Crime Indices report of DC: Violent Crimes at 56.2 and Property Crimes at 63.9–both higher than the crime index in Chicago, Los Angeles, and New York.

She Who is Mighty, we plead that lawlessness surrenders to love from community care to nurture and individual responsibility not to harm one another. Our strength is depleted from responding to one tragedy after another.

Turn the enemy against themselves once again as you did for Jehosaphat and bless Your people with abundant goods and favor in return.

She Who Is Peace, astound the enemy of peace with people who praise and worship You, nevertheless.

She Who Saves, hear our unceasing prayers that you can and you will stem the numbers of lives lost to crimes of violence and flood love over the world, this nation, our district, our wards, and our homes. Asé. Amen.

Mental Health Awareness: On this Side of Heaven

Some days I only have a mind to lament my condition like the Psalmist (22:14-15, NCV): *"My strength is gone, like water poured out onto the ground, and my bones are out of joint. My heart is like wax; it has melted inside me. My strength has dried up like a clay pot, and my tongue sticks to the top of my mouth. You laid me in the dust of death."*

Teach me, O Lord, to walk in Your truth–about MENTAL ILLNESS.

Your truth is that on this side of Heaven, mental illness is not a consequence of sin–it is a condition of life one in eight people in the world live with a mental disorder.

Teach me, O Lord, to walk in Your truth–about DEPRESSION.

You didn't turn Your back on David as he languished (Ps 6:6-7): *"I am worn out from my groaning. All night long I flood my bed with weeping and drench my couch with tears. My eyes grow weak with sorrow; they fail because of all my foes."*

Teach me, O Lord, to walk in Your truth–about ANXIETY.

To the 40 Million Americans living with anxiety, *"tell those who worry, the anxious and fearful, Take strength; have courage! There's nothing to fear. Look, here—your God! Right here is your God! The balance is shifting; God will right all wrongs. None other than God will give you success. God is coming to make you safe."* (Isa 35:4 TV)

Teach me, O Lord, to walk in Your truth–about COGNITIVE DISORDERS.

For even though Jeremiah (20:14) cried out–*"Cursed be the day I was born. . .why did I ever come out of the womb to see trouble and sorrow and to end my days in shame?"* –God esteemed Jeremiah as the last prophet to plead repentance over a nation!

Teach me, O Lord, to walk in Your truth–about EATING DISORDERS.

Women are twice as likely as men to embody an eating disorder. *"So, my dear family, this is my appeal to you by the mercies of God: offer your bodies as a living sacrifice, holy and pleasing to God. Worship like this brings your mind into line with God's. What's more, don't let yourselves be squeezed into the shape dictated by the present age. Instead, be transformed by the renewing of your minds, so that you can work out what God's will is, what is good, acceptable, and complete."* (Rms 12:1–2 NTE)

Teach me, O Lord, to walk in Your truth–about COMPASSION TOWARDS THOSE LIVING WITH MENTAL ILLNESS.

People living with mental illness often suffer in shame, are subjected to ridicule, and are the whispered topics of judgment. BUT, as for you, *". . . as God's chosen people, holy and dearly loved, clothe yourselves with compassion* [when a friend is depressed], *kindness* [when a stranger has a public meltdown], *humility* [in the presence of one whose self-esteem is vacant], *gentleness* [when food is the enemy instead of sweet fellowship], *and patience* [when grief has no expiration date].*"* (Col 3:12 TV)

This, O Lord, is Your truth! –*"I am sure that neither death nor life, nor angels nor rulers, nor things present nor things to come, nor powers, nor height nor depth, nor anything else in all creation, [including Mental Illness] will be able to separate us from the love of God in Christ Jesus our Lord."* (Rms 8:38–39 ESV) *Asé. Amen.*

Washington DC Emancipation (16) "We the People of DC" 2024

Sigh –Thirty years ago, then Delegate Elenor Holmes Norton voiced the unspoken: DC is a people obligated to taxation, though without representation comparable to the 50 states of this nation. Today, the Congresswoman's H.R. 51 bill is heard and affirmed by the Democratic-led House, though it remains scrutinized by the Republican-controlled Senate.

> *God who leads us to pray for those in authority over us, hear our weary prayers for justice for "We the People of DC."*

"We the People of DC" are Black and people of color who comprise the majority demographic of the District's 700,000 residents. DC Statehood *is* about racial justice.

> *Lord, may our Senators realize that in a democracy, justice for one is justice for all.*

DC Statehood might have been the vision of our ancestor and abolitionist Frederick Douglass, as his work and words bear witness to this movement: "Power concedes nothing without demand."

> *"We the People of DC," demand equality comparable to our tax per capita. Lord, in Your mercy, hear our prayer.*

Opposers to DC Statehood feign an unconstitutional bias to the H.R. 51 bill based on its 68.34-mile geographical plot, all while pretending that the 48 contiguous states (plus Alaska and Hawaii) are Indigenous homelands which the same Constitution allowed to be taken and claimed.

However, since the earth is the Lord's and the fullness thereof, the world and everyone in it, we pray for God's move of uncommon favor on the hearts of those on Capitol Hill.

Lord, in Your mercy, hear our prayer for uncommon favor to dismantle the filibuster resistance. May the power grab coveted by both sides be used to ultimately do what is right and righteous.

"We the People of DC" demand that the Black and people of color populations are not eradicated from pursuits of life, liberty, and justice. Lord, in Your mercy, hear our prayer.

Washington, DC is so much more than the White House, the Capitol, or the National Mall. "We the People of DC" is home to voters–a majority who are Black and people of color who have sustained the commerce and infrastructure for over 200 years of taxation without representation.

Lord in Your mercy, we seek wisdom on how to proceed with righting this wrong. Sustain grassroots foot soldiers protesting in the heat.

Lord in Your mercy, we pray for Congress to remain tenacious and for the Senate to concede to righting this wrong. Maintain the advances made by bill H.R. 51 in the halls of justice.

Lord, in Your mercy, DC Statehood is a chapter in Black history. In our history, we *always* give you glory! We the people of DC, #WeAreDC #51for51. Asé. Amen.

Easter and Eastertide

Jesus Is . . . Alive!

Hallelujah! Christ is risen as he said he would!
   Hallelujah! Jesus is alive!
Three days ago, it didn't look like Love would win.
   But, Hallelujah! Jesus is alive!
We listened to our Savior's dying declarations and heard him take his last breath.
   But, Hallelujah! Jesus is alive!
We watched the Holy Lamb of God's battered, broken, and bloodied body swaddled again–but this time in a burial shroud–and placed in a tomb hewn in a rock.
   But, Hallelujah! Jesus is alive!
We waited and wondered, "What happened?" all night Friday night. We waited and wondered, "What now?" all day Saturday. We waited and wondered, "What's next?" all night Saturday night.
   But, early Sunday morning, when the women got to the tomb to anoint his body, an Angel of the Lord proclaimed, "He is not here. He has risen as he said he would!"
Hallelujah! Jesus is alive!
   And Mary Magdalene, one of Jesus' disciples, saw him first and ran to tell the other disciples,
Hallelujah! Jesus is alive!
   The others came to witness the folded shroud and empty tomb, and they ran to spread the good news,
Hallelujah! Jesus is alive!

And since that day, and on today, we who believe in the Risen Lord proclaim this truth, "Hallelujah, Jesus is alive! He is alive, indeed!" Asé! Amen!

Resurrection: Call to Worship

The Holy Week ball has been in play
At the 3rd quarter Triumphal Entry, Jesus is ahead
It looked like an easy win at the last-play Last Supper

But what an upset when Judas betrays Jesus for the turnover
Satan is on the offense advancing downfield
with a touchdown in view

First down, the "Hosanna" crowd now cried, "Crucify him!"
Second down, walked-on-water Peter denied him
Third down, the disciples dessert him
(but the women surround him)

The clock is running out
While Jesus and the home team were hanging out,
waiting out the offense's next play
They were rehearsing Redemption's playbook

The state-sanctioned executioners huddled.
For the touchdown acceleration
The enemy could taste the touchdown celebration.

Arms stretched wide, pierced in his side,

Jesus hung his head and died
Touchdown!
Death, Hell, and the Grave danced in the end zone!

With the touchdown on the board
A guard on the opposing team protested
"Truly He is the Son of God!"

This late flag caused the referees to check the instant replay
All night Friday night, they reviewed Death's inbound/out-of-bounds possession
All day Saturday, they debated whether Hell scrimmaged on the inside or outside
All night Saturday night, they scrutinized the Grave's final call

But early on Sunday morning
Penalty flags were replaced with folded shrouds in an empty tomb
Turns out, Satan did not have possession of Jesus like he thought he had

That Friday celebration proved to be premature
And this Sunday, a Risen Christ erased Friday's score
And replaced a final score—Redemption won!

On Friday, I told y'all, that Sunday was coming!
Christ is Risen as he said he would!
Christ is Risen indeed!

Raised

"Praise be to the God and Father of our Lord Jesus Christ! In his great mercy he has given us new birth into a living hope through the resurrection of Jesus Christ from the dead." (1 Peter 1:3)

Hallelujah! Christ is risen! Hope is alive!

Jesus said, "I am the resurrection and the life. The one who believes in me will live, even though they die; and whoever lives by believing in me will never die. Do you believe this?'" (John 11:25–26)

Yes, Lord Jesus, we believe!

"For this is the will of my Father, that everyone who looks on the Son and believes in him should have eternal life, and I will raise him up on the last day." (John 6:40)

So we look to Jesus, the author and finisher of our faith.

"Who is to condemn? Christ Jesus is the one who died—more than that, who was raised—who is at the right hand of God, who indeed is interceding for us." (Romans 8:34)

We are raised above all condemnation!

"Therefore, if anyone is in Christ, the new creation has come: The old has gone, the new is here!" (2 Corinthians 5:17)

In Christ, we practice new ways to love one another.

"If you confess with your mouth that Jesus is Lord and believe in your heart that God raised him from the dead, you will be saved." (Roman 10:9)

Lord help those who have yet to believe and receive them into the family of God.

"With great power, the apostles continued to testify to the resurrection of the Lord Jesus. And God's grace was so powerfully at work in them all." (Acts 4:33:)

Preach preacher! Teach teacher! As often as we remember, we will tell the Resurrection story!

Hallelujah, Christ is risen, indeed! Asé. Amen.

Eastertide: Anticipation

Wait for the Lord; be strong, and let your heart take courage; wait for the Lord! (Ps 27:14)
> **O, how well we know about waiting—about anticipating answered prayer!**

When our hearts grew weary of waiting, God sent us song.
> **We sang hymns and spiritual songs, old-school jams and jazz, and prayers and protest songs.**

When we felt our hope had died in Winter, God sent the Spring.
> **We bore unimaginable grief waiting for a verdict, God's report came: Guilty! Guilty! Guilty!**

We were excited to see familiar faces, chat with visitors, and welcome new members.
> **While clergy and lay leaders stepped up and stepped in, God sent us a preaching, teaching, loving pastor.**

And, we never got tired of waiting for this good news—Pastor Young has finally arrived in the States!
> **Yes! While anticipating all of what we longed for, we hoped in God and God alone.**

So, Stay with God! Take heart. Don't quit. I'll say it again: Stay with God. (Ps 27:14, The Message) Asé. Amen.

Ascension Day

Divine Creator, Lifter of our heads, and Raiser of our spirits,
On this holy day of Ascension, we turn our eyes to the heavens
Where Your Son rose in glory, trailing clouds of light and majesty.

Just as the disciples stood in wonder,
We too stand in awe of Your power to elevate
That which was earthbound into the realm of spirit.

As Christ ascended, breaking the bonds of earth,
So too may our hearts rise above our daily struggles,
Lifting like smoke from sacred fires toward Your divine presence.

We are Your children, both of heaven and earth,
Standing with feet planted in the soil of our ancestors
While our spirits soar toward Your eternal kingdom.

Grant us the wisdom to understand
That as Christ rose, He did not leave us orphaned,
But promised the Spirit that connects all things.

May we, like eagles riding thermal winds,
Rise above the limitations of flesh
To glimpse the glory of Your eternal realm.

And as we walk this earthly path,
Let us remember that we are both dust and divinity,
Both human and holy, both mortal and meant for more.

In the name of the One who ascended,
Who reigns in power, and who will return in glory,
We lift this prayer to the highest heights.

Asé. Amen.

Pentecost

21st Century Upper Room Experience

Welcome All to this 21st Century Upper Room experience.

**We wait on something more than hot-air preaching
but are poised to receive a fresh move of God's ruah through us.**

We are not here for manufactured fire,
we are a peculiar people and holy nation

Gathered on a summer Friday night to be alight anew with fire from Heaven, individually and collectively to witness to the world that God is still speaking!!

And when Pentecost had come—welcome to this virtual upper room.

Pentecost: Suddenly!

YHWH the Holy One of Isreal, Jesus the Palestinian Jew, and Holy Spirit the Paraclete—we pause from pressures, problems, and proceedings to give You place to receive our praise.

We gather from the safety of our homes into the sanctuary of Your presence to hear from Heaven and help us heal the land.

In Your sovereignty, unction those who need a revival to tune in on purpose and stumble upon this broadcast by accident.

By Your grace, reveal salvation to others from spiritual ambiguity to experience the best of all there is in Christian community.

By Your Word, Water, and Sacrament, sanctify us holy anew to extend love without limits to the least of these whom You highly esteem in the Kin'dom.

YHWH the Holy One of Isreal, Jesus the Palestinian Jew, and Holy Spirit the Paraclete—you are welcome in this virtual place to hold a tangible place in every song sung, prayer prayed, hand raised, word uttered, and yeah and amen from our homes.

When it's preaching time, fill the preacher with all the time she needs to move us from knowing how to tell time, knowing when it's in Your time, and whatever is next in time!

Open our ears to heart and quicken our hands to obey Your Pentecost SUDDENLY this day!

Asé. Amen.

Trinity Sunday (Sunday after Pentecost)

In the lingering flames of Pentecost,
We gather in the mystery of Three-in-One.

Creator God, Ground of Being,
Who shaped worlds from void and stars from darkness,
Who breathed life into dust and possibility into emptiness,
Your power pulses through every heartbeat and sunrise.

Christ, Eternal Word made flesh,
Who walked our earthly paths with weary feet,
Who blessed our bread and shared our tears,
Your hope shines through every moment of healing.

Holy Spirit, Wild Wind of Heaven,
Who swept through the upper room with fire,
Who still moves among us like a mighty storm,
Your courage strengthens us for service.

Divine Trinity, Three Persons, One God
In this season after Pentecost,
As we contemplate Your threefold nature,
Make us instruments of Your triune love:

**Creators of justice,
Bearers of reconciliation,
Vessels of transforming power.**

We invoke Your presence among us now,
Perfect One-in-Three and Three-in-One,
Holy, holy, holy Lord,
God in Community, Divine Trinity.

**Through time and eternity,
World without end,
Asé. Amen.**

MAY

Mental Health Awareness Month

May is Mental Health Awareness Month.

There are options for how mental illness afflicts and arises within us, but

May we never forget that waking up in our right mind or even with a medicated portion of mental health and strength—God does good things for us!

Bless the Lord, Oh my soul—Let all that we are praise Your holy name!

Mothers Like . . . Me!

Mother God, Co-Creator of Heaven and Earth, fowl of the sky, fish of the water, of vegetation of the land, of the enigma of air, of the mystery of seasons, and of all who dwell therein–we have come home in Your bosom to worship.

> **You have shown us that motherhood is a complex calling. Being born from a mother is, for some, the extent of their encounter with motherhood.**

We honor these for whom–by nature, nurture, necessity, or intentionality–this day creates a quandary or distress.

> **We acknowledge their options and affirm their choices. Asé.**

We honor Mothers like **Eve**: ones from whose wombs generations are born and whose name is called First.

> **We honor Mothers like Mary: single mothers who hide divine messages in their hearts and take action instead of sitting in pity over their circumstances.**

We honor Mothers like Hannah: mothers over 40 who did not give up on praying to conceive and once she did, confounded others when she kept her promise to you!

> **We honor Mothers like Peninah: mothers who got laid but were never fully loved; mothers whose bodies bore babies only to serve the patriarchy.**

We honor Mothers like **Rizpah**: mothers of children slain in the streets who go on to give their lives to prevent vicious lies and systemic injustice from devouring truth.

> We honor Mothers-in-Law like Naomi: mothers whose faith outlasted misfortune and drew a daughter-in-law into covenant community and survival sisterhood.

We honor Grandmothers like **Eunice** and **Lois**: mothers who influence generations to serve God and follow Christ.

> We honor future mothers, pregnant mothers, new mothers, play mothers, church mothers, Adoptive Mothers, and Aunties who raise children like birth mothers.

We honor Mothers Like ***Shaddi*** – the Multi-breasted God: divine mothers of love who invest in children of the world, of the nation, of neighborhood schools, of next door, in their bloodline, and out in the streets. In them, no child is hungry, homeless, or left behind.

> We honor mothers for whom mothering was contentious and joyless, abusive and burdensome, embarrassing and inconvenient, alienating and abandoning; and we pray that they know by Your steadfast love they are understood and forgiven.

First and finally, we honor You, Mother God! You who made us in Your image, redeemed us from sinful consequences, and *reclaimed* us children of God and co-heirs to the Kingdom with Christ! Hallelujah! Asé! Amen!

When Mama Was God

When Mama was God
    She made miracles happen
    In the middle of a Houston ghetto
    The center of my universe, indeed.

    She walked on water
    In three-inch heels, matching bag
    With us five kids in her footsteps.

    She taught us to fear not.
    Night lightning, thunderstorms
    Hard work, new things, good success.

When Mama was God
    She created not one but two
    Fancy Easter dresses and sewed
    Lace on my socks to match.

    She hollered for me from the porch
    Compelling me to come out, come out
    From all my favorite hiding places.

She held me close with strong hands
So close that I would inhale
Warm fleshy bosom heat for air.

When Mama was God
She stood her ground with white folk
    Those blue-eyed devils of pure evil
    In the 60s. . . 80s. . . this new millennium.

She laid hands on us/me.
    So the cops wouldn't and trifling men couldn't
    Healing bad attitudes and broken hearts.

She made a dollar holler
On the occasions of more month than money
Without robbing anyone of anything.

When Mama was God
She blessed two fish and five loaves
    Or was that govm't cheese
    And canned mystery meat.

She kept an open-door policy
Always meant that somebody else
Would be sleeping on the living room floor.

She prayed for us and others
We eavesdropped, listening for our name
Knowing that no weapon formed against us would prosper.

When Mama was God.

"Girl, you just like your Mama,"
somebody said to me one day
when I was feeling a whole lot like God.

TRANSparent

(Trans- etymology: Latin prefix meaning "across", "beyond", or "on the other side of")

Might I be TRANSparent?
    I am a TRANSparent, and this
    Is my TRANSconfessional.

After nine months of hosting the TRANSgenic mystery
Of birthing a beautiful Black baby boy
I was TRANSformed from the
    TRANSient life of foster motherhood
into the TRANSfiguration of
    biological mother,
    blood-born Mama, and
    blessed Mommy

I became TRANSfixed on protecting my wombfruit
    from the unchecked TRANSgressions of the
    infamous badge-gun-baton blueGang
the TRANScultural hatred of luminous dark skin,
    TRANSaudient repulsion to esoteric kinked locs, and
    TRANSmitted envy of taller-than-most svelt gracefulness

He rebirthed *herself* as TRANSjective,
    ever negotiating her truth in the world
    a TRANSconjugant of soul and chromosomes

Just leaving home is the
    TRANSactional insistence on a thriving existence
Signifying TRANSwomanhood in stiletto nails and neon wigs
    TRANSmorgrifying concrete sidewalks into runways
    TRANSmuting childhood memories into museums
    And rebirthing my labored TRANSparency
        into her TRANSparent.

She eases into her TRANSedental self
    by TRANScribing a life that
    TRANSlates to healthy, whole, and multi-artistic

I ease into my TRANSparenthood with TRANScendent love
    queering the TRANSmutation of binaries
    at the TRANScept of salvation
TRANSmitting the Divine's truth that
    TRANS lives matter to our Creator, indeed.

I am the TRANSparent of *her*, and *she* calls me "Mommy."

Daughters of Zelophehad Must Have Been Womanists

What an outrageous notion
Such audacious acts
What to make of those courageous words
    Speak truth to power
    Speak truth to power
    Speak truth to power

Sho'nuff strong-headed willful behavior
Rejecting marginal good for magnificently better
Deliverance from my oppression liberates you too / you all
Responsible   for herself   her health   her wealth
In charge of   her satisfaction   her liberation
Serious about others when she has to be.
Yep, the Daughters (of Zelophehad) Must've been Womanist!

Women's Day: In the Beginning–God is a Woman!

In the beginning, God was woman, too. And when God made the human in God's image, she looked like you!
   In the beginning, God is woman, too!
In the Garden with Eve, or with Lilith from the depths of the Red Sea, woman has been since the beginning of history.
   Fact check: woman is not an afterthought, add-on, or appendage to man.
Is it a wonder that in woman wombs are the first homes of everything that has the breath of God within; and that through the mystery of gestation, we birth the best of all God imagines?
   God created woman and calls her "good"!
A woman's imagination is divine work whether as art or invention, recipes or fashion, dance that conjures healing and the erotic, and hairstyles hiding rice and maps to freedom.
   However, a woman's worth is in her mere existence, not only in her toil and labor.
Women are vessels of clay holding treasures of gold–the ways we show up, with quiet solemnity or loud, bodacious, and bold.
   (Women Only) Sister, which are you?
   (Men Only) Woman, I see you!
Woman, I am you, and you are me! Together we carry the Word of God forged in Holy Ghost fire, fulfilling our purpose with passion and the Armor of God as our attire:

Gold belt of truth and purple breastplate of righteousness, green shoes of peace and blue shield of faith, blood red helmet of salvation, and the illuminating sword–the Word of God!

Women's Day is a reminder that in the beginning, God is a woman, and today, we are God's women still; standing firm in the faith that keeps us in God's perfect will.

When women are celebrated, God is exalted. Happy blessed Women's Day.

Asé. Amen!

Women Honoring God in Word and Deed

In the beginning, God created the woman in God's image and likeness and called her "good."

> **The woman was *not* an afterthought or borrowed appendage. Can't you see God in me?**

Women live and move and have our being by the breath of God's divine imagination.

> **It is our reasonable service, then, that we let every detail of our lives glorify our Creator.**

So women, treasure every word you speak as apples of gold in bowls of silver!

> **Yes women, do housework and work-work with joy as unto God instead of man.**

And women, make time for your passions and creativity–unapologetically–like God did when creating you!

> **Women, turn to your neighbor and say "Rest!" *[pause and say it]***

Women, turn to another sister and say, "Rest!" *[pause and say it]*

> **People of God, turn to one another and say, "God rested, so *you* take time to rest from doing all the time!" *[pause and say it]***

We are a living sacrifice that every detail of our lives glorifies God, every day and in every way.

> **Women Only: In the name of our Creator, the love of Jesus, and the power of the Holy Spirit, we give thanks for being called "woman." Can't you see God in me?!**

All: Hallelujah! Asé! Amen!

Self-Rising Dough–Celebrating the Past and Living the Future

"If the part of the dough offered as first-fruits is holy, then the whole batch is holy; if the root is holy, so are the branches." (Romans 11:16 NIV)

Sometimes, I imagine God made me from Self-raising flour! Finely milled with leaveners to carry light and increase volume amidst the ordinariness of all creation.

Women: *God calls me "holy." I am Woman!*

Men: **She is Woman. Amen!**

I am Eve, the part of the dough offered as first fruits, yet, maligned for eating from a fruit tree.

Women: *God calls me "holy." I am Woman!*

Men: **She is Woman. Amen!**

I am Hagar. I saw God. God saw me. I first called him El Roi–God who sees. So, I endured being enslaved because God promised my son would be free!

Women: *God calls me "holy." I am Woman!*

Men: **She is Woman. Amen!**

I am Mary, a virgin girl risking it all to labor in an out-of-wedlock pregnancy, bear labor pains in unsanitary conditions for the whole world's salvation, and labor in grief at the foot of the Cross.

Women: *God calls me "holy." I am Woman!*

Men: **She is Woman. Amen!**

I am the Other Mary. I hear the whispers still about who I used to be, but Jesus picked me to preach Resurrection Gospel first!

Women: We are Self-Rising dough. Celebrating our holy past!

Men: **Amen!**

I am Sojourner Truth, a woman who saw dreams and had a vision of liberation. Some call me Black Moses, and I don't mind, but the difference is he asked for permission to let God's people go, whereas I gathered up my people and said, "Let's go!"

Women: God calls me "holy." I am Woman!

Men: **She is Woman. Amen!**

I am Anna Pauline Murray, but my friends call me Pauli. Before it was trending, I was a gender non-conforming, first Black woman Episcopal Priest in the United States, and a Civil Rights activist, lawyer, and theologian.

Women: God calls me "holy." I am Woman!

Men: **She is Woman. Amen!**

I am Katie Geneva Cannon, another "Black woman first" who was ordained by the Presbyterian Church (USA) but exiled to academia. Yet, in my exile from the mainline church, I became known as the Mother of Womanist Theology that transforms the church.

Women: God calls me "holy." I am Woman!

Men: **She is Woman. Amen!**

I am Christine Wiley, Delores Lynch, *and* Debra Camphor; Ancestor Deacons *and* Cathy Wilson; Mothers Lorraine Randolph, Clara Jenkins, Joyce Hooks, *and* Annette Canady; Tia with gifted hands *and* Jazmin with gifted praise. We are faithful women serving where sent and blooming where planted.

Women: God calls me "holy." I am Woman!

Men: **She is Woman. Amen!**

I am Katrina Carter, pastor and preacher. I am Lisa Dunson, denominational leader. I am LaKeisha Harrison, a bi-continental bridge between African Diaspora and Christian Theologies. I am every woman of God under the sound of my voice who is God's representatives in likely places and uncommon ways.

Women: We are Self-Rising dough. Celebrating our holy present!

Men: **Amen!**

Tamara, Elyse, and Erica; Jana, Henrietta, Kayla, *and* Jocelyn; Sydney, Simone, *and* Kennedi; Kameren, Da'Rya, *and* baby girls in arms and on the way–You are part of the dough that is rising in this church, in our community, in the Family of God! Because you are from the holy dough, you, too, are altogether holy!

Women: Daughters, God calls you "holy." You are our future in the Church and the world.

Men: **Amen!**

Sometimes I feel like God made me from Self-Rising flour. Offered up as a living sacrifice to sanctify the ordinariness of life. I am holy. The women before me are holy. The women beside me are holy. The girls who follow us are holy.

Let the women say: **Celebrating our past, thriving in this present age, and promised hope and a future, God calls us "good." God calls us "holy." We are Woman!**

Let the people say: ***Asé. Amen!***

African Liberation Day (25)

O God of our ancestors, who led the Israelites from bondage,
Who heard the groaning of Your people under Pharaoh's yoke,
We remember Your mighty hand in Africa's liberation struggles.

From Cape to Cairo, from Senegal to Somalia,
For the martyrs of African liberation and
The prophets who walked among us, we thank you.

For Archbishop Desmond Tutu's fearless voice,
For Julius Nyerere's Christian socialist vision,
For Kenneth Kaunda's faithful leadership,
For the countless priests and pastors who chose
To walk the path of liberation theology,
Finding in Christ the ultimate liberator.

Today we stand in the twin streams
Of our Christian faith and African identity,
Remembering that You, Lord Jesus,
Found refuge on African soil
When Herod sought Your life.

Grant us wisdom to forge a future where African Christianity speaks with its own voice,

Where our children stand proud in their dual heritage, where the cross and the ancestor tree stand together in sacred conversation.

May the blood of the martyrs,
The prayers whispered in mission churches,
The hymns sung in freedom camps,
The rosaries clutched during liberation wars,

The scriptures that gave strength to resistance leaders, the dreams of our freedom fighters, and the prayers of our mothers continue to water the seeds of true liberation.

For Africa must be free
Not only in body but in spirit,
Not only in politics but in faith,
Not only in name but in truth.

In the name of Christ our Liberator, who breaks every chain,

And by the power of the Holy Spirit who hovered over Africa's ancient waters,
And sends fire upon African Americans as we claim our complete freedom.
Asé. Amen.

Armed Forces Day

Most High God, Guardian of Justice and Truth,
We lift up our Black sons and daughters in uniform,
Who serve with dignity despite the weight of double consciousness—
Defending a nation while still fighting for full recognition within it.
Remember, Lord, the legacy they carry:

The Buffalo Soldiers who rode the frontier,
The Tuskegee Airmen who conquered the skies,
The Montford Point Marines who stormed beaches,
The 761st Tank Battalion who broke through enemy lines,

And countless others who served with excellence
When excellence was denied its proper honor.
Watch over our Black service members
In every branch and rank today:

Those standing guard in distant lands,
Those sailing on darkened seas,
Those flying through storm-crossed skies,
Those healing the wounded in medical units,
Those maintaining the complex machinery of defense,
Those leading with the wisdom earned through generations.

Protect them, O God, from the twin battles they face:
The visible enemies before them,
And the invisible weight of systemic barriers.

Grant them strength when they must be twice as good,
Resilience when they face familiar shadows of bias,
And courage to stand tall in their truth.

Shield their families who wait and worry,
Their children who miss them deeply,
Their parents who placed flags in windows
And prayers in their daily bread.

Let them feel the pride of their ancestors:
The determination of Henry O. Flipper,
The courage of Dorie Miller at Pearl Harbor,
The leadership of Daniel "Chappie" James,
The excellence of Colin Powell.

May they know they are never alone when they stand their watch,
That the prayers of the Black church rise with the sun to cover them in grace and power.

Lord of Hosts, bring them home safely
To a nation ever striving to live up to its promises,
To communities that honor their service,
To a future worthy of their sacrifice.

Until that day, grant them:
Wisdom in their duties,
Peace in their hearts,

Strength in their spirits,
And justice in their cause.

In the name of the One who breaks every chain and lifts every bowed head, we pray.

Asé. Amen.

Memorial Day

Most High God, You who counts every sparrow's fall,
Who knows the location of every lost grave,
Guide us in this sacred work of remembrance.
For the Black soldiers buried in unmarked trenches,
Their dog tags stripped, their names erased,
Their bodies cast aside like shadows

We remember their sacred names,
O Lord, we reclaim their dignity.

For those discovered generations later,
In French fields and Belgian forests,
In segregated plots and forgotten corners

Restore their honor, Ancient of Days,
return them to their people.

For the families who never knew,
Who waited at windows year after year,
Who passed down stories of missing sons

Heal their generational wounds and
bind up their inherited grief.

For the 40th Infantry and the Red Hand Division,
For the Harlem Hellfighters and Buffalo Soldiers,
Denied honor in death as they were in life

We speak their valor into memory, we carve their truth in stone.

For those still waiting to be found,
Their bones mingled with foreign soil,
Their sacrifice hidden by history's silence

Guide us to these sacred places, help us bring them home.

For the archaeologists and researchers,
The DNA specialists and military teams,
Working to restore identity and dignity

Bless their holy work of recovery, light their path to truth.

For the contemporary Black service members,
Who still face the shadows of this legacy,
Who serve knowing this history

Grant them strength and justice, shield them from similar fate.

We pledge to honor these recovered warriors
    To speak their names with reverence
    To teach their stories to our children
    To guard their legacy with fierce love

Until all are found. Until all are named. Until all are home.

Let no soldier remain forgotten,
Let no sacrifice stay buried in silence.
Give us persistence in the search,
Wisdom in the recovery,
And grace in the reburial.

Until that day when all are accounted for,
When every family has their answers,
When every soul rests in honored ground.

In the name of the One who knows every name,
Who calls forth life from death,
And justice from truth,
We pray. Asé. Amen.

Ordinary Time

JUNE

African American Music Appreciation Month

For the field hollers and work songs,
Rising from cotton fields and chain gangs,
Carrying codes of survival and resistance
We honor the songs of our ancestors,
their rhythm flows in our blood.

Our music is our medicine.

For the spirituals that lifted spirits,
"Steal Away," "Wade in the Water," "Swing Low,"
Each note a map to freedom, each verse a prayer
Their melodies are our inheritance, their hope still lights our way.

Our music is our memory.

For the mothers of the blues,
Ma Rainey, Bessie Smith, Sister Rosetta,
Who turned pain into power and sorrow into strength
Their voices break our chains, their courage teaches us to sing.

Our music is our freedom map.

For the jazz giants who reshaped the world,
Duke and Satchmo, Bird and Miles and Trane,
Who bent notes toward freedom and improvised new dreams.
Their genius opens doors, their innovation shows us possibility.

Our music is our victory.

For the soul singers who voiced our movement,
Nina's rage, Aretha's demand for R-E-S-P-E-C-T,
James Brown declaring "I'm Black and I'm Proud"
Their anthems fuel our march, their truth speaks our power.

Our music is our medicine.

For the hip-hop griots and prophets,
Who turned turntables into pulpits,
Making street corners into sacred spaces
Their verses tell our story, their rhythm moves us forward.

Our music is our memory.
For all Black music yet to come,
Born from tradition but breaking new ground,
Carrying ancient wisdom into future songs
We cherish this living legacy, we guard this precious gift.

Our music is our freedom map.

From shout to symphony
From bebop to breakbeat
From the ring shout to the club
The spirit moves, the culture lives
And the song goes on

Our music is our victory.

We give thanks for this mighty stream of Black musical genius flowing from Africa's shore, through centuries of struggle, into tomorrow's triumph.

Let every heartbeat its drum
Let every voice lift its song
Let every hand clap its praise

For the music that saved us
For the music that raised us
For the music that makes us
For the music that is us.

Asé. Amen.

"We All, Everyone, Everywhere" Bernice Johnson Reagon / LGBTQI+ Solidarity

For a moment, let's imagine the resplendent heavenly celebration when the world's beloved peacemaker, Bernice Johnson Reagon, transitioned from right now into life everlasting.

> We say her name, Bernice Johnson Reagon, civil rights activist, resistance psalmist, and embodied peace in Sweet Honey in the Rock.

She harmonized in alto singing liberation in *Ella's Song*...

> "We who believe in freedom cannot rest until it comes."

...defining God's love of the whole wide world in *Would You Harbor Me?*...

> "Would you harbor a Christian, a Muslim, a Jew? A heretic, convict, or spy? Would you harbor a runaway woman or child? A poet, a prophet, a king?"

...and reminding us that we who believe in the Resurrection will not mourn her passing as those with no hope in "In the Morning When I Rise"—

> "In the morning when I rise / Give me Jesus / You can have all this world / But give me Jesus"

Her discography is vast, her lyricism is lasting, and we say Your Name, Bernice Johnson Reagon, our sister in the struggle and ancestor where there are no more questions.

> So, the next time we sing "We All, Everyone, Everywhere," she brings us closer to the reality of solidarity.

That a day like today, Solidarity Sunday, commemorating the untimely and violent deaths of LGBTQI+ siblings in Christ and in Creation, becomes a distant memory.

A distant memory of when transgender women were executed for their exceptional ways of being.

A distant memory of when masculine-of-center beings were accosted in the streets because their swag made insecure others mad.

A distant memory of when same-gender-loving families could not grow their families their way– by in vitro, natural, or adoption.

A distant memory of when human rights were not synonymous with the LGBTQI+ right to live unafraid that leaving our homes escalated our likelihood of becoming a statistic.

On Solidarity Sunday, we sing, "We All, Everyone, Everywhere," until the love of God becomes the international anthem of every person, of every people, in every land.

On Solidarity Sunday, we look to the hills of our faith where our Help comes from–the Maker of Heaven, Earth, and All Humans– to stop the violence and establish peace.

Peace on Earth, as it is in Heaven. Asé. Amen.

March on Washington

Sacred Keeper of Justice and Time, we remember that August day in 1963 when Your people gathered before Lincoln's stern face, filling this city with dreams of freedom. On these sacred grounds where King's voice rang out, where feet marched and hearts soared with hope, we stand now in the shadow of that mighty gathering, still seeking full citizenship, still demanding dignity.

Remember, O Lord, the bitter irony: that in this very city where hundreds of thousands marched for voting rights and human dignity, seven hundred thousand souls still cry out for basic representation, for statehood denied.

God of Moses who demanded Pharaoh, "Let My people go," hear the voices of District residents who pay taxes without representation, who send their children to war for democracy, while democracy stops at their own doorstep. We remember Marion Barry's fierce cry, "Free DC!" Eleanor Holmes Norton's relentless struggle, and license plates that proclaim our pain: "Taxation Without Representation."

From Shaw to Anacostia, from Howard University to Congress Heights, from the halls of power we clean, to the chambers where we cannot vote, Your people await justice. Lord of Frederick Douglass who made his home here, of Mary Church Terrell who fought segregation here, of Duke Ellington who gave us song here, make our struggle for statehood ring as loud as King's dream echoed that summer day.

May the spirit of '63 fuel our fight for '24. Let the legacy of that march give strength to our steps today until the capital of democracy finally knows democracy itself.

Until justice rolls down like the Potomac,
Until righteousness flows like Rock Creek,
Until the stars on our flag number fifty-one,
Until Washington is both free and home.

Asé. Amen.

Gun Violence Awareness

On January 21, 2013, Hadiya Pendleton marched in President Obama's second inaugural parade. One week later, 15-year-old Hadiya was shot and killed on a playground in Chicago.

Soon after this tragedy, Hadiya's friends commemorated her life by wearing orange–the color hunters wear in the woods to identify themselves and prevent accidental shootings of other hunters. #WearOrange is now observed every June to honor communities plagued by the proliferation of guns and to witness the impact of gun violence alongside families who live with this terror and survive this trauma.

Thousands of people wear the color orange to honor Hadiya and the more than 43,000 Americans killed with guns, and approximately 76,000 more shot and wounded annually. Today, our Covenant family wears orange as a symbol of solidarity and hope for a future free from gun violence!

LGBTQI+ Solidarity

God, our foundation, on who our faith pivots yesterday, today, and forever more, we gather on this Solidarity Sunday to make this offering of praise and worship to You–You are welcome in this place.

We gather like the colors of the rainbow, bearing witness to Your presence in our lives individually and in community.

May all who worship with us in person, online, or by providential accident open their hearts to see one another as the family You have made us.

We have come into Your house to be equipped to act justly, love mercy, and walk where You walk among the marginalized, hurt, and hopeless.

Lord God, delight in every song and amen, in every offering and prayer, in every hug and encouraging word, in the people and in the preacher.

Bless be the ties that bind our hearts in Your love. In Jesus' name, we pray. Asé. Amen.

LGBT+ Solidarity

On this Solidarity Sunday, remind us that we are one human family formed out of Your imagination. May all who mourn the loss of life or injury of an LGBTQ+ loved one due to violence just for living in their being that reflects Your ingenious creativity of humanity find refuge in an affirming church and comfort in You.

May our solidarity not just be a concept but a lived reality. Help us to see Your face in every person we encounter, to love our neighbors as ourselves, and to work tirelessly for a world that reflects Your kingdom of justice, peace, and love. Asé. Amen.

LGBTQ+ / BLACK PRIDE: Litany of Celebration "Out on the Hill"

Gather here. Gather now. Gather everyone. Mother-God welcomes you with arms wide open!

Lesbians & Gays: I'm here!
Straights & Questioners: I'm here!
Bis & Trans: I'm here!

One: Out there we often give in to fear by only sitting with those who look like us, worshipping with those who believe like us, and the exclusion serving only those who agree with us. But today we commit to survival and wholeness of entire people!

Women (Cis & Trans):
> We are committed to survival and wholeness of entire people, male *and* female.[1]

Men (Cis & Trans):
> We are committed to survival and wholeness of entire people, male *and* female.

---

1. Alice Walker's Definition of a "Womanist" from *In Search of Our Mothers' Gardens: Womanist Prose* (1983).

All: We are committed to survival and wholeness of entire lesbian, gay, bisexual, transgendered, queer, intersexual, celibate, questioning, discovering, and straight.

One: While in here, in the presence of Divine, we commit to lay down what makes us different and keeps us estranged. While out there this week, OUT on the Hill, we commit to *each* becoming the *other* so that we *all* can become God's *one*.

Left Side of the Room:
> We are committed to survival and wholeness of Christians, Muslims, Jews, Atheists, and others' spiritual paths; rich, poor, and working-class;

Right Side of the Room:
> We are committed to survival and wholeness of— Republicans, Democrats, Independents, Greens, partisan, bi-partisan; and yes, even of pets, our companions.

This week we convene in our nation's capitol, one body with many parts, putting faces on policy from the Hill to the hollows, influencing justice for more than just us from the White House to the house next door, and educating for equity for an entire people.

ALL: May we Love with arms wide open, work for survival that is just, and seek wholeness that welcomes everyone!

Pastoral Installation: Litany of Celebration

(For The Reverend Dr. Shelley Denise Best)

Gather here. Gather now. Gather everyone. Mother-God welcomes you with arms wide open!

Many *Black*: I'm here!
Many *White*: I'm here!
Many *Others*: I'm here!

Out there we often give in to fear by only sitting with those who look like us, the convenience of worshipping with those who believe like us, and the exclusion of serving only those who agree with us. But today we commit to survival and wholeness of entire people!

***Women*: We are committed to survival and wholeness of entire people, male *and* female.**[1]

***Men*: We are committed to survival and wholeness of entire people, male *and* female.**

***LGBTQI and Allies*: We are committed to survival and wholeness of entire people, male and female: lesbian, gay,**

---

1. Alice Walker's Definition of a "Womanist" from *In Search of Our Mothers' Gardens: Womanist Prose* (1983).

bisexual, transgender, queer, intersexual, celibate, questioning, discovering, and straight.

While in here, in the presence of Divine, we commit to lay down what makes us different and keeps us estranged, and we commit to *each* becoming the *other* so that we *all* can become God's *one*.

Left Side of the Room:

We are committed to survival and wholeness of entire people—Christians and Muslims and Jews and others; rich and poor and working-class;

Right Side of the Room:

We are committed to survival and wholeness of entire people—Republican and Democrat, Independent and Green, partisan and bi-partisan; and yes, even of pets, our companions.

Today we celebrate our beloved sister, one who is committed to survival and wholeness in the Church, in her community, and of *others* better known as, entire people!

She teaches us to Love arms wide open, working for survival that is just and wholeness that welcomes everyone!

[A Call to Worship Experience by Rev. Raedorah C. Stewart ©2011]

Fathers' Day: Our Father, On Earth as He is in Heaven

When Jesus, our elder brother, taught the disciples to pray this way:

Our Father in Heaven, holy is Your Name...

We learned the blueprint of the divine purpose and esteemed privilege for men to be called Father, Abba, Daddy, Big Daddy, Stepfather, and Adopted Father.

Thy kin'dom come on Earth as it is in Heaven...

Imagine for us the possibilities of fatherhood emulating sacrificial love and eternal security.

Give us this day our daily bread...

Instructs fathers to provide shelter, food, and clothing; lavish child support in money and the things money cannot buy; shows up for daughters who play sports and for sons who dance ballet; teaches his children the five love languages by word and deed.

Forgive our transgressions to model how to forgive those who transgress against us...

If quick-tempered, may fathers be quicker to apologize, slower to anger, more gentle in correcting, and very patient in teaching.

Lead us not into temptation, but deliver us from evil deceptions and stereotypes...

Sons of fathers who abandoned and betrayed them may be tempted to repeat these behaviors. However, we pray that men *choose to* repent from being deadbeat dads, in child support arrears, and blaming mothers for the fathers' sins visiting upon the sons.

For You, Our Father, are the kin'dom, power, and glory...

Show fathers how to lead community, love family, and *earn* due respect when they follow You.

Today, we celebrate men who become fathers after Your heart, O God Our Father. Turn their hearts back to their children–whether by birth, adoption, or community–today and forever.

Asé. Amen.

Gun Violence (7)

Most High God who hears the cries in our streets, who counts every fallen sparrow, who knows every mother's tears by name, we cry out for our District, our communities bleeding.

For every child who walks to school in fear, every teenager who's learned the sound of gunfire before learning to drive, every grandmother who's lost another grandson—we cry out for mercy.

In Southeast, in Northeast,
On Martin Luther King Avenue,
On Good Hope Road that needs Your hope,
On Alabama Avenue calling for angels,
The shell casings tell stories of despair.

Remember, O Lord, our beloved dead:
The children playing on porches,
The fathers walking home from work,
The mothers caught in crossfire,
The teenagers whose dreams died on corners,
Their names are sacred on our lips.

[Invite congregation to call names.]

We remember Maurice Scott,

We remember Karon Blake,
We remember Carmelo Duncan,
We remember all our children whose names become hashtags and headlines, whose futures were stolen by bullets.

God of the Peaceable Kingdom, how long must Black mothers dress their children in funeral clothes? How long must we count bodies instead of diplomas? How long must we fear the night?

We cry out against the systems that flood our streets with guns while starving us of resources. That offers thoughts and prayers while denying us power and change. That blames the victims while protecting the profiteers.

Transform, O Lord:
The rage into restoration,
The trauma into triumph,
The pain into purpose,
The grief into governance,
The bullets into books,
The violence into vision.

Until our streets echo with laughter,
Until our children know safety as birthright,
Until our elders can sit on their porches in peace,
Until the sound of gunfire is replaced by the music of life.

Protect our young ones,
Guide our lost ones,
Heal our wounded ones,
Comfort our grieving ones,

Strengthen our serving ones,
Remember our fallen ones.

For the District, for every Black community living under the shadow of the gun,
We pray for deliverance, we demand change, we claim healing.

Asé. Amen.

Juneteenth (19)

By the waters of the Atlantic, where Ancestors rest, we remember and honor their names.

> **Asé, we remember**

For the drums that kept beating, the songs that kept humming, our rhythms survived the Middle Passage.

> **Asé, we survived**

Through the Orishas, who walked with us in chains
Through Yemaya, who protected us in the waters
Through Oshun, who kept love flowing in our hearts
Through Shango, who preserved our dignity
Our spirits remained unbroken

> **Asé, we carry their power**

For those who ran to freedom
By North Star, through swamp, over mountain
Guided by African wisdom, protected by ancestral spirits
Their footsteps mark our sacred path

Asé, we follow their way.

When word reached Texas
On the nineteenth of June
Our people filled churches and fields with praise
Freedom rang through the land

Asé, we were transformed

For the feast tables we set
With black-eyed peas for good luck
With okra carrying memories of Africa
With watermelon sweet as liberation
With red drink poured for ancestors' blood
We feast in remembrance

Asé, we celebrate

By the ring shout of our elders
By jumping the broom of our unions
By the naming ceremonies preserving our ways
We keep tradition alive

Asé, we persevere

Through Gullah wisdom and Geechee ways
Through Negro spirituals and freedom songs
Through Black church and hush harbors
Our culture could not be stolen

Asé, we maintain

For today's children who must know
The price of freedom, the power of memory
The strength of African ways in American soil
We teach, we tell, we testify

Asé, we pass it on

We are the children of those who would not die
We are the dreams of those who would not break
We are the voice of those who would not be silent
We are African, we are American

We are the keepers of both worlds

May the ancestors dance with us today
May the Orishas light our way forward
May the elders' wisdom guide our steps
May the children learn our sacred stories

**May freedom ring louder with each passing year
Until justice rolls down like mighty waters
And righteousness like an ever-flowing stream**

Asé. Amen.

JULY

Independence Day: What Freedom?

They sing about sweet liberty
While our people still ain't free
July 4th rings hollow here
When justice isn't drawing near

What freedom, what freedom?
Ask my brother in the cell

What freedom, what freedom?
Ask my sister raising hell

What freedom, what freedom?
'Til all chains disappear

What freedom you talking 'bout?
It ain't reached down here

They wave their flags up in our face
While we're still fighting for our space
Their independence sure came true
But we're still waiting on breakthrough

What freedom, what freedom?
Ask my brother in the cell

What freedom, what freedom?
Ask my sister raising hell

What freedom, what freedom?
'Till all chains disappear

What freedom you talking 'bout?
It ain't reached down here

Disabled Pride

O Divine Creator who knit us in our mothers' wombs, who shaped each nerve, each synapse, each difference with purpose, we are wonderfully made

> **Each body sacred, each mind holy.**

For our wheels that dance, for our hands that sign, for our minds that process differently, for our bodies that move in unique rhythms, we are fearfully and wonderfully made

> **Our souls know this truth deeply.**

You know our sitting down and our rising up, whether by lift or ramp, cane or crawler, whether fast or slow, smooth or shaky, You understand our ways

> **You celebrate our adaptations.**

Your thoughts toward us are precious, each stim a prayer, each accommodation a blessing, each assistive device a tool of divinity, how vast is the sum of Your acceptance

> **How wide is Your embrace.**

You have searched us and known us in our chronic pain and fatigue, in our sensory differences, in our mental divergence, we are known completely

We are loved absolutely.

Before our tongues can form words, whether we speak, sign, type, or tap, You know exactly what we mean, You hear every voice

You understand every silence.

Where can we go from Your acceptance? In psychiatric wards or therapy rooms, in rehabilitation centers or group homes, Your love follows us there

Your pride in us never ceases.

Even the darkness is light to You, our invisible disabilities, our masked conditions, our hidden struggles, You see us completely

You honor our whole being.

We reject the shame others would give us
We claim the pride that is our birthright
We honor the bodies that carry us
We celebrate the minds that guide us.

For we are not broken. We are not wrong. We are not less.

We are as we were meant to be:
Sacred in our difference
Holy in our variance

Divine in our divergence
Perfect in our imperfection

**Our disabilities are not burdens to bear,
but paths to deeper wisdom**
Not flaws to fix, but ways to be whole

May we always know our worth
May we always claim our space
May we always celebrate our truth
May we always honor our ways

**Until all bodies are seen as holy
Until all minds are known as sacred
Until all ways of being are celebrated
As reflections of divine diversity**

Asé. Amen.

AUGUST

Seasons Change: What Do You Need Most?

Our Mother, Our Father, God of seasons and situations, Lord of light and love, Spirit of comfort and power, we call to worship every willing and wanting heart here today.

On the eve of Summer ending and Fall routines beginning, let us get back to business with Your blessing.

But let us not get so consumed with busyness that we fail to meet You in daily prayers and intercessions.

In our busyness, nudge us to stop and see You in leaves changing, water tables rising, and harvesting nightshades.

In our bustling to return to classrooms and public transportation, may kindness and courtesy be the new normal for those who once took them for granted.

In our busyness, may we find refuge and rest on Sunday mornings online, and use wisdom and prudence on Sunday mornings' return to in-person worship.

In our bustling, show us how to share and not hoard in preparation for another expected wave of this national health pandemic.

In our busyness, when we eventually get exhausted and overwhelmed with this change in season, remind us that You give power to the faint and strengthen the powerless.

On the eve of living into a post-quarantine new normal, make us aware that the old normal was not pleasing in Your sight. May our going back to business be more of a blessing than of a burden, more just and more gentle, kinder and more benevolent.

Asé and Amen.

Faith / Yes!

O God Embodied, the one made flesh who dwelt among us, help us to arrive this morning with a "yes."

A "yes" to our faith that says our bodies are good and holy, just as and however they are.

A "yes" to show up here, even if our minds may be in other places at times.

A "yes" to believing enough in You, this community, and our own call to know this is where we need to be in this moment.

A "yes" to bringing all that comes from and through our hearts to You, O Heart-maker.

Come, let us bring ourselves to God's table of plenty.

With our inherent worth and dignity to guide us. Selah.

Asé. Amen.

SEPTEMBER

National Black Family Reunion Month

Spirit of our Ancestors, Keeper of Sacred Bonds,
Watch over every car, plane, and bus
Carrying our people home to this reunion ground.
Wrap Your arms around every traveler
From the four directions of this land.

We call on the ancestors who kept family ties
Through slavery's separation,
Through Great Migration scattering,
Through urban renewal displacement—
Guide our people safely to this gathering place.

Shield the coolers packed with love,
The covered dishes wrapped in foil,
The sweet potato pies and mac and cheese,
Each fork full of memory,
Each plate carrying heritage.

Remember those missing from our circle:
The ones working who couldn't come,
The ones behind prison walls,
The ones estranged by hurt,
The ones resting in Your glory.

Grant us:
Joy in our gathering,
Peace in our differences,
Grace in our conflicts,
Strength in our bonds,
Hope in our future.

We call on:
The spirit of our great-greats who survived the ships,
The courage of those who fled slavery by night,
The wisdom of those who built Black Wall Streets,
The determination of those who marched for freedom,
The love of every Black parent who made a way.

By the power of the ancestors,
By the strength of the elders,
By the hope of the children,
By the love of the family,
We gather, we remember, we continue. *Asé. Amen.*

Family Reunion: Roll Call

Bless the grandmothers coming with photo albums,
Heavy with memories and lost faces,
Bless their hands that will touch young heads,
Speaking names of those gone on,
Connecting threads of memory to new cloth.

Watch over the elders carrying family stories,
The aunties with secret recipes,
The uncles with hidden histories,
The cousins meeting for the first time,
The children learning their roots.

Heal the wounded places in our family tree:
The branches broken by addiction,
The leaves scattered by incarceration,
The roots stressed by poverty,
The buds crushed by violence.

Bless our LGBTQ+ family members
Coming home with their full truth,
Our adopted ones finding their place,
Our step-children and half-siblings,
All blood of our blood, heart of our heart.

Pour healing into family wounds,
Turn bitter roots sweet,
Make old hurts into wisdom,
Transform trauma into strength,
Let love cover all.

Let every child present
Feel the weight of their inheritance,
The pride of their bloodline,
The love of their people,
The strength of their roots.

May this reunion be:
A healing ground for old wounds,
A learning space for our young,
A resting place for our weary,
A celebrating place for our victories,
A planning place for our future.

Let every hug heal, every tear cleanse, every story teach,
Every laugh lighten, every dance free!

Asé. Amen.

National HBCU Week

Gracious God of Knowledge and Legacy, we celebrate these sacred grounds of learning where Black excellence was born and nurtured when other doors were closed.

For Howard's hills touching the sky,
For Morehouse molding men of might,
For Spelman's sisters rising strong,
For Hampton by the rolling sea,
For Tuskegee's towering legacy,
For every HBCU standing proud—we lift our voices in gratitude.

Remember, O Lord:
The study sessions in ancient halls,
The mentors who believed when none would,
The scholarships built from pennies and dreams,
The research that changed the world,
The hands that lifted while climbing.

Bless now:
Every pledge seeking purpose,
Every chapter doing service,
Every student burning midnight oil,
Every professor planting seeds,
Every alumni giving back.

Alpha Phi Alpha, men of distinction, we honor Your gold and black.

Alpha Kappa Alpha, the First Black Greek sorority to light the way, Your ivy still grows, still glows.

Kappa Alpha Psi, excellence unfolding, Your diamonds still shine with achievement.

Omega Psi Phi, lifting up scholarship and perseverance, Your brotherhood lifts as you climb.

Delta Sigma Theta, marching for suffrage, standing for justice, Your sisterhood transforms the world.

Phi Beta Sigma, doves of peace, Your blue and white lights the path.

Zeta Phi Beta, scholarship beyond measure, Your blue and white brings healing.

Sigma Gamma Rho, raising the standard, you are gold and royal blue excellence.

Iota Phi Theta, building a tradition, Your brown and gold shows the way.

Let the legacy continue:
Through each step show and stroll,
Through each community project,
Through each scholarship fund,

Through each mentoring moment,
Through each call for justice.

May our colleges remain:
Fortresses of knowledge,
Temples of culture,
Harbors of hope,
Forges of leadership,
Gardens of dreams.

And may our Divine Nine remain:
Strong in their purpose,
United in their service,
Steadfast in their mission,
Bold in their vision,
Faithful to their founders.

Until every dream is achieved,
Until every mind is freed,
Until every path is opened,
Until every star is reached,
We serve, we study, we soar.

For the culture,
For the legacy,
For the future,
We gather.

Asé. Amen.

Deaf Awareness Week

Note: *This litany is meant to be spoken and signed simultaneously in ASL.*

Holy One who created both thunder and silence, who speaks in still small voices and visual vernacular, we celebrate the beauty of ASL, the poetry of signing hands, the dance of Deaf praise, the wisdom of Deaf culture. When worship excludes our Deaf siblings, we are all diminished,

Our praise is incomplete *[Sign: WORSHIP MISSING PIECE].*

When interpreters stand in sacred space, when Deaf hands shape the word of God, when silence speaks louder than sound, God's love speaks every language and

The Spirit moves in fullness *[Sign: SPIRIT MOVE FREE].*

In this sacred space when we sign "Jesus Loves You," we sign "Welcome Home," and we sign "You Belong Here," our hands speak love

Our hearts beat as one *[Sign: TOGETHER ONE].*

We commit to breaking down barriers of exclusion by making space for signing choirs, training interpreters for ministry, learning basic signs for welcome, understanding Deaf culture and

We promise to change and grow *[Sign: PROMISE CHANGE GROW].*

Bless these hands that shape prayers in the air, dance with scripture's truth, sign songs of praise, tell God's story in silence. and bridge worlds of sound and silence.

Make us truly one body *[Sign: IN CHRIST ONE BODY].*

May God's love be shown in every sign
May Christ's peace be felt in every touch
May the Spirit dance in every gesture
Until all can say and sign:

We are one in worship
We are one in spirit
We are one in love
[Sign: ONE LOVE FOREVER]

Asé. Amen. *[Sign: AMEN]*

OCTOBER

Breast Cancer Awareness: Quiet Killer, Silent Pain

(for sisters who have survived or succumbed to breast cancer and the people who love them)

We probably first heard it as we quietly sat
Alongside her headstone, why was that?
From a mouth that always laughed out loud,
Why was this secret kept as a shroud?
This quiet killer came with silent pain;
And she won't be here to laugh, again.

Every time we lose another,
It could be some sweet child's mother.
And more than just one life will be lost,
Needlessly, and with such great cost.
This quiet killer with its silent pain;
Kept a child from being loved, again.

As we remember her and that last cup of tea
We silently hope the next one's "not me."
All the while wishing we could just yell it out;
"What in the world is this all about?"
This quiet killer and silent pain;
That won't give us time together, again.

Sisters, we're hurting and dying, too.
Brothers, we need you to help us through.
Don't let us die, not in the prime of life,
We've got years to be a friend, a mother, a wife;
Although this quiet killer and silent pain,
Treats our lives with utter disdain

Today, we need you to make a choice,
To give this killer and pain a voice.
Today let's learn, tomorrow let's share,
To give hope and promise in place of despair.
So that this quiet killer and it's silent pain,
Won't take our women in numbers by name.

Domestic Violence Month

For those trapped behind closed doors, living in the shadow of raised fists, whose bodies bear invisible wounds: God of refuge, hear our prayer.

"The Lord is a refuge for the oppressed, a stronghold in times of trouble." (Psalm 9:9)

For the children who learn to read anger, who count footsteps and hold their breath, who know too well the sound of breaking, Tender Shepherd, shield their souls.

"He will cover you with his feathers, and under his wings you will find refuge" (Psalm 91:4)

For those who were told they deserved it, whose spirits were crushed with cruel words whose sacred worth was denied and trampled, Spirit of Truth, restore their dignity.

"You are precious and honored in my sight, and I love you" (Isa 43:4)

For those who cover bruises with makeup, who explain away broken bones, who smile through trembling lips, God of Liberation, break their chains.

"The Spirit of the Sovereign Lord is upon me. . .to bind up the brokenhearted, to proclaim freedom for the captives" (Isa 61:1)

For communities that turned blind eyes, for churches that preached silence and submission, for those who chose comfort over justice, Lord of Truth, we repent.

"Learn to do right; seek justice. Defend the oppressed" (Isa 1:17).

For abusers who hide behind scripture, who twist love into control, who make a mockery of sacred vows, God of Justice, convict their hearts.

"Better a millstone hung around their neck than to cause one of these little ones to stumble" (Luke 17:2).

For advocates on the frontlines, for shelters offering sanctuary, for counselors holding space for healing, Source of Strength, sustain their work.

"Let us not become weary in doing good" (Gal 6:9).

We declare together:

Your body is sacred
Your spirit is precious
Your voice matters
Your life has value
Your safety is paramount
Your healing is possible
Your future is worth fighting for.

We commit to:

Breaking the silence
Believing survivors
Supporting escape
Funding shelters
Changing laws
Teaching consent
Stopping violence before it begins.

Most Holy Protector, guard those in danger tonight, guide those seeking escape, and strengthen those who advocate.

Heal those who carry scars, transform those who harm, until all may dwell, in the shelter of Your peace.

Asé. Amen.

Diversity, Equity, Inclusion, & Belonging

For every voice unheard, every story untold, every identity unseen, we create space for truth to bloom, we open circles wider still until all find their place.

"There is neither Jew nor Greek, slave nor free, male nor female, for you are all one in Christ Jesus." (Gal 3:28)

For those who navigate ramps and stairs, who read with fingers and speak with hands, who process the world uniquely, we adapt our ways, we remove the barriers until access is a birthright.

"The Spirit of the Lord is upon me . . . to proclaim good news to the poor, freedom for the prisoners, recovery of sight for the blind, to set the oppressed free." (Luke 4:18)

For the rainbow of languages and cultures, for the symphony of beliefs and traditions, for the mosaic of ways to be human, we celebrate difference, we honor each journey until diversity becomes strength.

"After this, I looked, and there before me was a great multitude from every nation, tribe, people, and language, standing before the throne." (Rev 7:9).

For those denied fair chances, blocked by systemic walls, carrying generational wounds, we dismantle oppression, we redistribute power until equity flows like water.

"Learn to do right; seek justice. Defend the oppressed. Take up the cause of the fatherless; plead the case of the widow." (Isa 1:17).

For those who code-switch to survive, who mask their true selves, who shrink to fit others' comfort, we make room for authenticity, we protect sacred identity until belonging is guaranteed.

"For You created my inmost being; You knit me together in my mother's womb. I praise You because I am fearfully and wonderfully made." (Psalm 139:13–14)

For the wisdom of elders, the energy of youth, the insight of excluded voices, we listen deeply, we change direction, until all wisdom guides us.

"Do not cast me away when I am old; do not forsake me when my strength is gone . . . Even when I am old and gray, do not forsake me, my God." (Psalm 71:9,18).

For the future we dream, where every child thrives, where no one stands alone, we do the work, we hold the vision until beloved community arrives.

"The wolf will live with the lamb, the leopard will lie down with the goat . . . They will neither harm nor destroy on all my holy mountain." (Isa 11:6,9).

We commit our hands to justice, our hearts to change, our minds to growth and our souls to love; until every table is round, every circle is whole, and every voice sings free!

"Let justice roll on like a river, righteousness like a never-failing stream!" (Amos 5:24).

May we build bridges, not walls. May we open doors not close them. May we share power not hoard it. May we heal wounds not cause them.

Until the human family reflects divine diversity, in all its sacred glory. "How good and pleasant it is when God's people live together in unity!" (Psalm 133:1).

Asé. Amen.

National Coming Out / Welcome In Day (11)

Divine Creator of Rainbow Beauty, who made diversity in Your image, who blessed love in all its forms, and who calls us each by our true names, we celebrate those made in Your image regardless of others' desire to disparage their being.

For every closet door opening, every truth finally spoken, every self finally claimed, we celebrate your courage, we honor your journey–You are beautifully made!

For our transgender siblings, living boldly in their truth, claiming their sacred names, we see you, we affirm you–you reflect divine glory!

For our queer youth seeking safety and acceptance, finding their way home to themselves, we embrace you, we protect you–you are precious and worthy!

For our elders who survived, who fought and marched and died, who made this path possible, we remember you, we thank you–your legacy lives on!

For our bisexual family, for our asexual kindred, for our non-binary beloved, we celebrate your wholeness, we honor your complexity–you expand our understanding of love.

For our intersex community, whose bodies remind us that diversity is divine design, we learn from you, we stand with you–you teach us sacred truth.

For all who love differently, who express uniquely, who live authentically, we rejoice in your presence, we need your light— you make our family complete.

In God, Love is love, gender is sacred, identity is holy, expression is divine, family is chosen and given, community is life-giving, and acceptance is non-negotiable.

As God's church, we commit to opening every door, widening every circle, blessing every union, protecting every child, supporting every family, honoring every story, and celebrating every identity.

Until every church is affirming, every home is welcoming, every space is safe, every heart is open, every love is honored, every self is sacred, and every spirit soars free.

Grant LGBTQIA+ persons the courage to come out (if and when they choose), grace to welcome in, wisdom to support growth, power to protect truth, and love to transform the world.

May every coming out be a coming home, every revelation be met with celebration, and every truth be wrapped in acceptance; until all of us are free to be fully, gloriously who God created us to be.

Asé. Amen.

Stewardship: "Be the Miracle" Capital Campaign

This is God's house. We are stewards of the vision, mission, *and* building! May God never inquire of us, *"Is it a time for you yourselves to dwell in your paneled houses, while this house lies in ruins?"* (Hag 1:4)

> **Lord, may the miracle of giving guide my giving above my regular tithes and generous offerings so this house will not fall into utter ruin.**

We boldly ask that You would "enlarge our territory" (1 Chron 4:9) as we reciprocate by giving to enhance the functionality of this building–our headquarters to refuel for outreach and be revived within!

> **Lord, give me the courage to give sacrificially to the reopening of a state-of-the-art industrial kitchen, inspected and approved, and freed to serve our members and the masses.**

We long to participate in the miracle of your mathematical mystery, like when Jesus' disciples lamented, "We have only five loaves here and two fish." (Mt 14:17), and yet, when that little lunch was blessed and broken, it fed over 5,000 men, along with women and children, and they left with to-go plates!

> **Lord, give me the wisdom to trust those given charge over managing the miracle.**

We pray for our pastor, trustees, and finance team to remain honest in their counting, shrewd in their investments, knowledgeable about contracts and contractors, and transparent in spending so that every cent is accounted for, and every bill is accountable.

Lord, I want to be a part of the miracle of the restoration of this house, Your house, so its future glory casts shade over its former glory.

We *are* the miracle–individually and collectively–of God's faithfulness to meet every one of our needs (Phil 4:19) as we tend to the needs of this building that serves the congregation and the community.

All: We are the Miracle in our giving in this season for the sole reason of making God's house glorious and glory-filled! *Asé!* **Amen!**

COVID-19: *Requiem*

Divine Healer of Body and Soul,
We remember the empty chairs,
The last FaceTime calls,
The hands we couldn't hold,
The funerals we couldn't attend.

We honor healthcare warriors
Who stood in death's shadow,
Our essential workers who risked all,
Our elders taken too soon,
Our communities devastated.

Grant us wisdom to trust science,
Courage to protect each other,
Strength to keep masking when needed,
Faith to believe in healing,
Hope to see beyond this valley.

For every long hauler,
Every grieving family,
Every struggling survivor:
Pour out Your healing balm.
Let us rebuild, together.

Asé. Amen.

NOVEMBER

All Saints Day (1)

Who do we remember on All Saints Day?
We remember the prophets of justice:

**Dr. King who had a dream,
Malcolm who taught us wisdom,
Fannie Lou Hamer who sang freedom songs,
Harriet who followed the North Star.**

Who do we remember on All Saints Day?
We remember the keepers of culture:

**Maya who caged birds sang,
James Baldwin who spoke truth to power,
Toni who told our stories,
August who staged our lives.**

Who do we remember on All Saints Day?
We remember the healers:

**Rebecca Lee Crumpler, first Black woman MD,
Mary Seacole who nursed the wounded,
Daniel Hale Williams who mended hearts,
The midwives who caught our babies.**

Who do we remember on All Saints Day?
We remember the teachers:

Mary McLeod Bethune who built colleges,
Septima Clark who taught citizenship,
Carter G. Woodson who preserved our history,
Anna Julia Cooper who lifted as she climbed.

Who do we remember on All Saints Day?
We remember the church mothers:

Who starched the altar cloths,
Who made communion bread,
Who taught Sunday School,
Who prayed without ceasing.

Who do we remember on All Saints Day?
We remember the music makers:

Mahalia who sang the gospel,
Duke who composed elegance,
Nina who screamed freedom,
Miles who birthed cool.

Who do we remember on All Saints Day?
We remember our own beloved dead:

The grandmothers who plaited our hair,
The fathers who worked two jobs,
The aunties who kept family secrets,
The children gone too soon.

We remember them all:
The named and unnamed,
The famous and forgotten,
The celebrated and silent,
Those who marched,
Those who martyred,
Those who made a way.

They surround us like a mighty cloud,
Their blood runs in our veins,
Their dreams live in our hearts,
Their work continues in our hands.

Until we meet again,
At the welcome table,
In that great getting up morning,

We remember.
We honor.
We continue.

Asé. Amen.

Veterans Day (11)

Divine Commander, we honor our Black veterans who served with dignity while fighting two wars–one abroad and one at home. Remember those who wore America's uniform but couldn't sit at its lunch counters, who defended democracy but were denied its promises, who came home to continue the fight for civil rights.

We celebrate the Tuskegee Airmen's excellence, the Buffalo Soldiers' courage, the Montford Point Marines' determination, the 761st Tank Battalion's power.

Protect our Black service members today who still face the double burden of serving while Black. Heal their wounds, both visible and hidden, honor their sacrifice, and grant them the full measure of respect they have earned.

Asé. Amen.

Black Adoption (18)

Most Holy Creator, Who sets the lonely in families (Psalm 68:6), we lift up the 112,000 Black children waiting for adoption, the 23% of our children overrepresented in foster care, and the sacred souls seeking forever homes.

Remember the families opening their hearts, for "I have called you by name, you are mine" (Isa 43:1).

Bless the Black families who, despite being only 14% of the population, adopt at higher rates within our community, understanding that we must care for our own.

Guide the 40% of Black children in foster care, let them know they are not forgotten statistics but precious seeds of promise, for "Before I formed you in the womb, I knew you" (Jer 1:5).

Strengthen the adoptive parents who step forward, though Black families are often overlooked by agencies, though we receive less support and face more scrutiny,

Still, we answer the call to love another's child as our own, for "Love bears all things, believes all things, hopes all things, endures all things" (1 Corinthians 13:7).

Support the birth mothers making painful choices, the 62% of Black children who enter care due to neglect, often poverty mislabeled, systemic barriers misunderstood.

Hold them in Your grace, for "Can a mother forget her nursing child? Though she may forget, I will not forget you" (Isa 49:15).

Bless every Black family choosing to adopt, every social worker fighting for our children, every mentor supporting our youth, every community member extending care.

For we know "God places the solitary in families" (Psalm 68:6), and we are all called to this holy work.

Until every Black child has a home, until every family has support until love conquers system and circumstance,

We pray for our children, for as scripture promises, "I will not leave you as orphans" (John 14:18). Asé. Amen.

Note: Statistics sourced from the Administration for Children and Families, U.S. Department of Health and Human Services, and the National Council for Adoption.

Transgender Day of Remembrance (20)

Loving and living God, Creator of the heavens and the earth, the cosmos and great waters, and every living thing, creature, and being–we dedicate this service to those made in Your image who have succumbed to violence spurned by hatred of those whose identities flow along the compendium of transgender, non-binary, and otherwise gender non-conforming.

In You, we all live and move and have our being. In You is our worth to be loved, not hated; to live safely, not always afraid; and to be routinely celebrated, not annually memorialized.

At Covenant Baptist United Church of Christ, we are a people striving to live into the Great Commandment to love You with all our heart, and with all our soul, and with all our mind.

And this Transgender Day of Remembrance is our offering of obedience to love our neighbor as we love ourselves.

In this moment, we pause to call the names of transgender, non-binary, and other gender non-conforming family, friends, framily, House families, club community, bar regulars, elders, and youth murdered–at any time–but especially since this time last year.

[The congregation should call the names of those we remember.]

Our transgender, non-binary, and other gender non-conforming siblings are made in Your divine imagination! Open the eyes of all humanity to witness Your wonder through them.

Open lawmakers' minds to be law-keepers that secure access to transgender healthcare and protect their lives in the streets. Civil rights movements and human rights legislation must include transgender rights.

Open the hearts of those who fetishize them–drawn to their exquisite selves while simultaneously loathing their attraction to ones You created and called "Good." Transform those hearts from murdering our siblings to keeping their not-so-secret secrets.

Open the doors of the Church universal as we have opened them at Covenant to welcome, include, appoint to leadership, receive their gifts and talents, and become a part of the Beloved Community without limitations.

May we continue to uphold the Great Commandment to love You, ourselves, and one another through every way others show up! Asé. Amen.

Adoption! God's Family Plan

November is National Adoption Month! By the power of the Holy Spirit of adoption, we rejoice that we are the family of God and we celebrate adoptive parents and adoptive children with great joy!

By the power of the Holy Spirit of adoption, we are privileged to call God our Father, God our Mother, and one another kin in Christ!

[Adoptive Parents and Families] *Just as God is father to the fatherless, it is easy for us to adopt children into our hearts and homes by papers, by proximity, and by predicaments.*

[Adopted Children and Siblings] *Although forsaken by earthly fathers and birth mothers, we are grateful that God sets the lonely in families who picked us to love as their own!*

Some parents adopt blood-kin like Mordecai who positioned Hadassah to save a whole nation of kin from annihilation. Aunts who become *Mama* and Uncles who become *Daddy* may very well be a child's answered prayer.

Other parents adopt children like Pharaoh's daughter who found Moses and raised him as her own! Children by adoption are God's answered prayers!

When Jesus called those who do the will of God his brothers and sisters and mother, he fashioned for us a kinship birth by faith and covered by the Blood, eternally.

[**Adopted Parents and Children**] *We thank God for setting the model of 'chosen family' before us and for the sacred call of becoming 'family!'*

> *All*: **The Spirit testifies that we are the children of God. Adopted by faith in Christ Jesus, our Elder Brother, we are made children of God, indeed** *Hallelujah! Asé! Amen!*

Thanksgiving: "God Gives Godself"

When it's prayer time at CBUCC, we are bold enough to believe in God who answers prayers—immediately, timely, and eventually. It is with this assurance that God hears prayers from this place—the place of your heart—that we petition God to once again, give to those who earnestly seek God. Let us pray.

Creator God. Elohim. Maker of heaven and earth. Source of love and salvation. Presence of peace and power.
    We worship You, for You alone are worthy of our praise.
        Heaven, hear our petitions, intercessions, and supplications as witness that we glory in Your Name.
Lord, hear our prayer.

For being Adoni, Lord of Your people in whom there is no longer Jew or Greek, male or female, slave or free
    In the insidious wake of racism, sexism, classism, and ableism, we ask nonetheless that Your will be done on earth as it is in heaven
    With confidence in Your mighty hand to save,
    we offer thanks for the hope there is in our work for equality and equity,
    and we glory in Your timing that makes all things beautiful.
Lord, hear our prayer.

For being Jehovah-Jirah, God who provides
> Despite people living in food deserts and being poisoned by contaminated water supplies, we implore Your power to heal the hearts of those who exploit the land.
>
> With assurance in Your ability to make a way out of no way
>
> We offer thanks for shelter, food, and clothing and for tangible, spiritual, and relational needs;
>
> Sanctify anew food bank to stave hunger one meal at a time and clothing drives to dress children for school and anywho need it from the elements.

Lord, hear our prayer.

For being Jehovah-Rapha, God who heals
> Even in this liminal space of the global COVID-19 pandemic that ravishes those on the margins of society while equity of access to health care is being debated
>
> Yet, we assert that You have given knowledge and wisdom to those in authority over individual and communal wellness to formulate effective vaccines and establish protocols to defeat this virus.
>
> We offer thanks with testimonies of being cured, praise reports of Negative test results, and joyful songs of mass inoculations; and, we glory in that You revive us when weary and renew our strength when we are weak while reaching those uncertain still about arresting this adversary to global health and well-being.

Lord, hear our prayer.

For being Jehovah-Shalom, God our peace
> Even in the furnace of Black body sacrifices by self-appointed white supremacists, in You we resist with laughter, music-making, giving birth, and building justice legacies.
>
> We give You thanks for going before us in the ongoing war for justice, mercy, equality, inclusion, and equity; and we glory

in Your peace that causes us to resist with self-care in the mornings and rest with good sleep through the night.
Lord, hear our prayer.

And so, on this Thanksgiving Day, together with the Psalmist we sing (139:17–18), *How precious to me are Your thoughts, O God! How vast is the sum of them! If I would count them, they are more than the sand. And when I awake, I am still with you.*

Most earnestly, we pray that our petitions align with Your promises, and our intercessions enter the holy of holies, and that our supplications are summed up in the sentiments of the simple song: Thank You. Thank you, Lord. We just want to thank you, Lord! You've been so good! So good! You've made a way! When we couldn't see a way! We just want to thank you, Lord!

In the name of Jesus and the witness of our ancestors delight in our prayer, Oh God. Asé! Amen!

Thanksgiving for Africans in America (nee African-Americans)

(for four readers)

Thanksgiving holds a complex and nuanced meaning for African Americans, reflecting both historical pain and resilience. While the traditional narrative of the holiday celebrates a peaceful feast between Pilgrims and Native Americans, many African Americans view the holiday through a more critical lens that acknowledges the broader historical context of colonization, slavery, and systemic oppression.

Africans stolen to the Americas became for their captors enslaved people whose bodies might have been deprecated, yet whose minds remained liberated.

Pilgrims in our thanksgiving prayers were not praised nor protected from the imprecatory prayers of our deep groans and loud wailing.

While colonizers feigned benevolence in giving us a day off, it was for them, a self-serving day of decadent gluttony and exercise in cognitive dissonance.

African Americans are most vocal in spreading a growing awareness of the holiday's problematic historical roots. We recognize that while the traditional Thanksgiving story romanticizes early colonial interactions, this narrative glosses over the brutal realities of Native American genocide and the subsequent enslavement of African people. The arrival of European settlers ultimately led to devastating consequences for Indigenous populations and was part of a system that would later support the institution of slavery.

While the colonizers feasted, First Nations people mourned their genocide from diseased gifted blankets and musket executions.

While the colonizers feasted, enslaved Africans plotted our escapes to a freedom the soul imagined for our babies.

While the colonizers feasted upon exploitation of our lives, we set our face towards the deliverance that the Great Emancipator would bring! Not Lincoln. We are talking about the Lord!

Thanksgiving for Africans in America is not monolithic. This day encompasses joy, pain, reflection, and hope—a microcosm of the complex African American experience in the United States. Some of us even choose to observe a National Day of Mourning, which coincides with Thanksgiving Day, to honor the indigenous peoples who suffered tremendous loss during colonization. Many focus on the holiday's potential as a time of healing, reconciliation, and community building.

Our giving thanks is a testimony to God's faithfulness generations past, despite present, and hoped-for future.

Our giving thanks remember our Ancestors whose bodies bore stripes while tied to trees–very much like Christ Our Redeemer endured.

Our giving thanks resounds with gratitude and the cacophony of kin coming together for food and fun, and even sets the lonely in f(r)amilies of new friends among old neighbors.

Our giving thanks is worship. The kind of worship from our thinking of the goodness of God that compels us to start thanking God for God's faithfulness day after day!

Our giving thanks banks unseen blessings and unmerited favor.

Our giving thanks is joy-filled as we emulate great feasts by distributing food baskets in our community where food scarcity transcends race, gender, and class.

Our giving thanks is a sacrifice of praise in our DNA for ancestors who escaped or died trying; for human rights leaders seeking civility rooted in love; and for waking up with a reasonable portion of health and strength for today's journey!

On Thanksgiving, Africans in America (nee African-American) set tables laden with roasted fowl and baked hog, sweetened vegetable and tart nut pies, hand-picked greens and snapped peas, and cast-iron cornbread dressing seasoned until the Ancestors call it enough, and give God thanks for lives lost so long ago and lives waiting to be born into our legacy.

Thanksgiving for Africans in America is a holy day, not merely just another holiday. And so, we give thanks to God who is on the side of the oppressed, who stands against the oppressor, and whose heart lavishes humanity with love! Asé! Amen!

Pastoral Prayers for the People

Praying People

Praying people are a peculiar breed
Discerning spirits and feeling needs
To those who may not understand
We prefer anointing with oil and laying hands
    we bind and loose, touch and agree
    we gather together with two or three
    we stand in the gap so none will perish
    we war in the Spirit for those most cherished
    we pray through the night or with the sunrise
    we pray hands lifted up and with tears in our eyes
Praying people don't wait to pray on cue
Praying people pray because that's what we do!

Asafetida (Acifidity) Bags and Prayer Cloths

(For Rev. Dr. Sista Linda Hollis)

whatever ailed you she held the cure in hand
from the right pocket of that worn gingham apron
curative herbs and anointed rags
prayer cloths from the mail and asfiddity bags

sometimes when she is praying tears
she had a little help with her fears
baby's colic /cold /whooping cough
my moody blues /miscarriage /menarche
all called for the same remedy
    Lawd, have mercy!
    Hear me now, have mercy!
    Mercy suits my case right now!

and a pinch of asfiddity
baby's by tincture rub on the belly
mine's bitter gum in a shot of whiskey
sometimes crushed fine in distilled water tea
    Lawd, have mercy!
    Hear me now, have mercy!
    Mercy suits my case right now!

baby and me we fell asleep to the sound of her prayers
scraps of prayer cloth pinned to our gowns
the bitter herb boiling in our blood
awakened some time later
both felt a whole lot better

was just thinking about woman
with the dozen years issue
of spent, bent, and bleeding body
> *Lawd, have mercy!*
> *Hear me now, have mercy!*
> *Mercy suits my case right now!*
why did no one string up a pouch of asfiddity around her neck?
guess it wasn't necessary
after all it was the Prayer Cloth Who was her Healing.

[Asfiddity is the common name of the African plant Asafoetida. A foul-smelling, bitter gum made from the dried sap of the plant was a staple in Southern folk medicine for its preventative and healing properties. Big Mama used it all the time. Mama used it sometimes. I could use some, right now.]

Solidarity Sunday: Call for Permanent Cease-Fire

Lord, we need You now, we need You now–every second, every minute, every hour, of every day–we need you.

Our hearts are heavy, yet hopeful, for we hope in You to hear our prayers, pleas, and petitions. Some come out as words, the ones that flow as tears, especially those that form as groans too deep for words.

> God is our healer, and we lift all those sufferings in body, mind, or spirit. While You comfort them with the promises of Your presence, guide the hands and hearts of caregivers, and grant wisdom to those seeking tested cures and trial treatments. We lean on You, Creator, to restore and bring wholeness.

God of all nations, we seek Your presence in a world that is increasingly fractured and overwhelmingly uncertain. Where humanity's darkness seems to favor genocide, shine Your light of justice and swift intervention. Protect the vulnerable, comfort the grieving, and stir the world's conscience to action to preserve life. Help us never to be silent in the face of such evil and keep our Pastor in his bold stands in the valley of the shadow of death here and abroad.

Sovereign Lord, in these times of political turbulence, be our steady rock. Appoint leaders after Your heart that pursue wisdom, integrity, and the common good.

Compel citizens to eagerly engage peacefully in protest and be visible in voting to preserve the democratic process. Where there is party division based on hate and greed, succumb to a love that lands us on common ground and shared purpose.

Prepare our ears for the preached word and our hearts for those seeking You or a church home. We pray this in the name of the One who taught us to love one another,
In the name of Jesus, Asé. Amen.

In Expectation: Waiting for a Pastor

Oh Lord, have mercy, mercy suits our case right now.
> We have laid at Your feet, love and lament, give us faith to leave all that concerns us in Your hands.

We are a people who know You answer prayers from this place, and here we are again, waiting in expectation for how You will heal and comfort even when death is the healer;
> Waiting in expectation for You to provide when the month is longer than our money

Waiting in expectation for You to establish peace in lands occupied by melanated people made in Your image burdened with genocide by those who have forgotten their Creator.
> Waiting in expectation for Your hand to save our children of every age and set as a sentry around Black men who deserve to grow old.

Waiting in expectation for Your kin'dom to come through us on earth as we participate in bringing heaven to the disposed, broken-hearted, and marginalized.
> Lord in Your mercy hear our hearts as we serve outside this house. Give us courage to love radically and wisdom to preach the gospel in our doing more than in our talking. Transform us into living epistles in the languages of this age.

Now, Lord, we lift the one appointed to this congregation and anointed to preach the whole counsel of God in word and in deed. Give him an instructed tongue to rightly divide the word of truth. Honor his submission as Your servant to bring us bread and his discipline as a scholar to break bread to feed and fill all who hear.

Preserve his body, mind, and spirit. Remind him of Your pleasure in his very existence.

We offer these prayers, believing that You hear our prayers and pity every grown and for as long as we live, we will hasten to Your throne.

In the name of Jesus, Asé. Amen.

God Almighty in Battle for Us

Mighty God. God Almighty in battle. God of Creation lamenting loss by the hands of men in power, and women co-signing, wars on humanity–whether on the front lines under fire or from podiums of propaganda—have mercy and hear our prayer.

- Israeli government genocide of Palestinians veiled as retaliation against Hamas
- Simultaneous, less coverage, genocides in Zimbabwe, India, Turkey Syria, and Ukraine

May the priests, prophets, pastors, and peacemakers who bear the word the Lord like the Arc of the Covenant at the Jordan, stand for justice . . . for peace . . . against Zionism . . . for humanity . . . on truth . . . in courage

- stand until mourning is turned into dancing . . . until the proliferation of arms is replaced with alleviation of homelessness . . . until childhood hunger is eradicated and nutrition is upheld as a basic human right . . . until every promise from Eden to the Judgement is yeah and amen.

Intercession for the Nations

It's not the posture of the body, it's the purpose of the heart that gets God's attention. For these on our prayer list, we pray for healing and comfort, peace and prosperity, and strength for their journey, today.

Let us also remember:

Maui: fires, loss of native residents, and evil land grab opportunists

Palestine: Israeli war crimes enacted to disrupt quality of life–namely destroying water wells

Africa: persecuted church in Nigeria and Somalia, drought in Uganda and Ethiopia, and African children hungering for food and education.

Sovereign God, hear our prayers.

Hear our prayers for names called aloud and those whispered in tears.

Hear our prayers for weary workers against evil in elected positions.

Hear our prayers for life and life abundantly for ourselves, our families, and humans everywhere.

Into Your hands, we commit our prayers for the everywhere, everybody, and everything. When we sing You have the whole world in Your hands, we pray that the earth and the cosmos come to delight in You instead of destroying what You have given to us.

Oh Lord, have mercy. Mercy suits our case right now.

Our hearts are overwhelmed with bad news from all four corners of the world; yet we hear You leading us to the rock that is higher than hurt, hate, and horrors of this world.

> Transform our tears into testimonies as Your will is done on earth as it is in heaven. We wait to see Your glory as we work to be Your peace.

Hear our prayers, Oh God.

Asé. Amen.

Kin in Christ

Jesus, high priest, incarnate prophet, elder brother, lover of our soul–by every one of Your Names we call on Your power to hear our prayers.

We pray for kin in Christ who mourn family members who have succumbed to the insidious virus wreaking havoc upon humanity. May their memories be precious and their tears sweet. May sudden adjustments accompanying such a great loss come with ease in discovering a new way of living. Lord, hear our prayer.

We pray for kin in Christ suffering from illness, infirmities, and chronic illnesses. Move through miracles and medicine to restore organic balances and move upon the hearts of medical professionals to serve with compassionate care. Lord, hear our prayer.

We pray for kin in Christ who are waiting and longing. Some are waiting for good news about a career, bank loan, a loved one to come home, housing to make a home, and college admission letters. Some are longing to love and be loved with creativity, reciprocity, and mutuality; longing to become entrepreneurs who operate in the black; longing to find an elusive inner peace that disallows joy to fill a void in their souls. Lord hear our prayer.

We pray for kin in Christ who are seeking You. Open their eyes to see You in the mundane and in the miraculous. Open their hearts to know Your love letters in sunrises and sunsets, in rain and seasons, in kindness of strangers, and strangers wearing masks. We pray they come to know Your love that loves them even while pursuing You. Lord, hear our prayers.

Lend Your ear oh Lord to our petitions and to our supplications. Holy Spirit continue to speak through this service that transcends space and depends on technology. Use our pastor's preparation to speak transformation in our living. Use the love that flows heart-to-heart and breast-to-breast whittle away at the extended isolation of following COVID protocols. Lord, hear our prayers.

Thank you for hearing prayers from this place. We rejoice with praise reports of recovery and restoration, reunification, and renewal. We rejoice just because morning by morning we are benefactors of Your blessings and vessel of Your mercy. Thank you, God, for teaching us to pray boldly, expecting You to keep Your word to do exceedingly, abundantly, above all we ask, desire, or imagine!

Lord, may our prayers soar to the heavens and reside there until they are answered Your way in Your time, in a way that blows our minds! In the name of Love, also named Jesus, Savior, and Redeemer.

Asé. Amen.

We Come in Confidence

This is the confidence we have in approaching God: that if we ask anything according to God's will, God hears us. (1 John 5:14)

The Most High God and Holy One of whom this season is named and this service reminded us to thank You for Your faithful presence in our lives and our congregation. Thank You for the gift of salvation, for the fellowship of believers, and for the privilege of serving You.

Lord, we acknowledge our shortcomings and sins. We have not always loved as You commanded, nor served as Your best representatives in the world. Forgive us for times of apathy, moments of doubt, and instances where we've failed to trust Your perfect will at work beyond our weakness. Hear our prayer, cleanse us from unrighteousness, and renew our spirits.

We pray for our congregation:

Each person: to grow in faith and receive more grace

Each family and chosen framily: to enjoy one another's company and be a source of comfort

Each member: discovers their gifts and callings as valuable to the vitality of ministry in and through this place

Each visitor and seeker: to know that we take hospitality seriously and that our welcome is sincere

Each leader: with grace to serve, mercy to share, and wisdom to mentor new leaders

Each minister: to serve in support of the vision You have given our pastor and to the needs of the people

Our pastor: humility and audacity to lead, seasons of contemplation and elevation to serve, integrity and discipline to study

We pray for our neighbors:

In Ward 8 Bellevue: preserve the legacy of a community that holds vestiges of the pride of Chocolate City in the wake of gentrification; stave displacement in the onslaught of development; restore pride in its people

Throughout the District: for the National Cathedral and benefactors to our Food Bank in this season of celebration and weekly sustenance for many in this food desert

In America: brace ourselves for what is unfolding as tyranny and unbridled theodicy; Lord, confuse the contractors of this chaos and turn them against themselves until they implode or repent

In Palestine, Gaza, and the West Bank: we stand in solidarity with peacemakers and are too familiar with the grief of the people; hear our prayers in tears and legislation

Next-door neighbors: may the overflow of our favor find its way into their homes as we witness by our lifestyle even more than by our words

We pray particular prayers for those affected by and infected with the HIV virus or AIDS (auto immuno-deficiency syndrome) disease. Compel us beyond this prayer to use wisdom in protection, detection, and integrity to prevent the spread of HIV among young people, gay people, hetero people, and infants.

May the power of Your blood discover a cure, comfort the sick, and give us courage to ask fewer questions and offer more love as we serve our siblings so impacted.

Most High God and Holy One, hear our prayer. We pray with the confidence to "not be anxious about anything, but in every situation, by prayer and petition, with thanksgiving, [we] present [our] requests to You [that Your] peace, which transcends all understanding, will guard [our] hearts and [our] minds in Christ Jesus. (Phil 4:6–7)

Please hear the prayers of Your people. We offer ourselves afresh to Your service. Use us as instruments of Your peace and witnesses to Your love. May everything we do bring glory to Your Name. In the precious name of Jesus Christ, our Lord and Savior, we pray. Asé. Amen.

Womanist Travels to Salvador, Bahia, and Accra, Ghana

Mother of Daughters who take their fass selves all over Your creation,
hear our prayers for traveling mercies, kindness of strangers who are creation kin,
and favor of governments in lands of the world organized through oppression.
We pray for protection at checkpoints and covering of angels whether sleeping or traveling in the cover of night. We pray for pure water, whole food, and strong bodies
to take hydration and nourishment to have strength for this journey. We pray that their witness leaves an impression that God dwells within and a fragrance of peace that transcends language and translates into every culture. Mother of Daughters who
take their fass selves all over Your creation, hear our prayers.
Asé. Amen.

Prayer for Mother in Distress at Childbirth

In the beginning, Oh God, in council with Son and Spirit, You created magnificence.

And even still before creation, before the foundation of the world was yet laid, You formed this Mother, her womb, and her child. As witnesses to her magnificence being created and called Your daughter, we gather by faith to dethatch Heaven's roof to lift her into Your healing presence.

Praying now that the trauma realized upon such a radical delivery be reknown as a miracle. We pray that Your healing is greater than an infection. We pray that Your peace quiets pain. We pray that no anxiety shall sound louder than her worship. We pray that her baby thrives through the affection of others available to hold, cuddle, swaddle, rock, soothe, and feed.

We pray for the hands that hold hers know that she is in Your hands—that place where her name is inscribed and her safety abides. Yes, God, we are wailing, weeping, and witnessing women, stand in the gap between grief and grace, praying to our Creator that You heal Your daughter and make whole this Mother, Wife, Lover, Daughter, Scholar, Sister, Friend.

In the name of Jesus, in the name of Jesus, in the name of Jesus, may "Amen" be our witness to Your word to hear prayers from this place.

Asé. Amen.

Clergywomen Prayer

Mother God / Father God of us all
Remind my brothers that I, too, am *imago Dei*
That being made in Your image
sanctifies, justifies, and qualifies me
to hold all offices of the Church
exercise all gifts for the Church
perform all duties in the Church
without apology. Lord hear our prayers.

O, Creator of Justice for all
Prompt my brothers to understand
That their idolatrous attachment to traditions
Denies, decries, and defies Spirit's work in me to
preach good news to the poor
comfort the brokenhearted
liberate any in captivity without apology.

Lord, hear our prayers.
Holy Trinity be our all
Teach my brothers that You hear my prayers
That the uncommon names I call
when I call on You
clarifies, magnifies, and glorifies

You to be also
Mother, Son, Spirit
Creator, Redeemer, Universe
Womb, Wound, Wind
without apology.
Lord, hear our prayers.
Asé. Amen.

We Lay Down Our Burdens

God Almighty, we lay down the burdens we have carried because You are here and witness You hearing prayers from this place.

> We call the names of Loved Ones
>> Comfort bereaved
>> Heal the sick
>> Sustain the suffering
>> Provide every need
>> Restore the fallen

We lay down the burdens we carry for. . .
> Neighbors next door to us, throughout the District, and especially in Belvue
>> May the grace and favor upon us overflow to them
>> May kindness be our first response towards one another instead of suspect and fear
>> May their housing not be threatened by greedy increases in rent, unfair mortgage lending, or sudden unemployment
>> May their cabinets be filled with staples and their refrigerators filled with fresh foods
>> May their homes be sanctuaries for all who reside there

We lay down the burdens we carry for...

Nation poised on the precipice of tyranny and demise of democracy

As the "idea of a plan" is being revealed as an insidious blueprint for evil to have free reign–even if only for a season

Protect immigrants who came by land that are criminalized, while immigrants flying in by air are pardoned

Thwart every effort to subject women to the perversion of misogyny and patriarchy

Be a fence around Black young people who are receiving texts from anonymous keyboard cowards threatening them with slavery.

Lord! Reassure our babies that this Auntie and the village are standing in the gap and on the front line to prevent this folly and foolishness!

We are our ancestors and are prepared to join them before our babies know the atrocities of white history.

We lay down the burdens we carry for...

International causes that violate human rights and inherent worth

Years have passed, yet we have not forgotten that genocide of brown bodies and black lives continues to be sport for a culture whose only fear is that they will become recipients of the evil they have done for generations

We've lost count of the names and are overwhelmed by the numbers of mothers wailing, holding dead babies, and fathers gone mad from groaning in grief

We pray for world leaders more interested in rigging elections instead of responding to staving another virulent strain of COVID and childhood diseases that have been all but eradicated through vaccines that are now being vilified

We lay down our burdens...
    In the presence of God, "Lay it Down!"
        In the name of Jesus, "Lay it Down!"
    In the power of the Holy Ghost, "Lay it Down!"

Asé. Amen.

Walking with God

Walking with God is remembering
laughing as a little girl
skipping three blocks home from Sunday School
singing a memory verse.

Walking with God is remembering
floating across matriculated stages
thanking God and Mama
for giving gifts and talents to excel
in poetry and pageantry.

Walking with God is remembering God
as my last thought under anesthesia's lull
and the surgeon's hand
to complete work on my heart
He created.

Walking with God is remembering
266 days of gestation for a perfect baby boy
conceived in love made in God's image.

Walking with God is remembering
giving birth as the city burned

washing soot from cartop and doorstep
abiding in peace
astounding me and
praying for enemy and friend.

The Holy of Holies

When in distress God's face one cannot see
He sends us to meet with them
In the blessed seat of the Holy of Holies.

As they come in seeking healing from You
It is for Christ's sake
We were called and given this work to do.

Bodies bruised and battered often by someone known
Come seeking refuge in a place
Where God's unconditional love would be shown.

Minds tormented by the enemy's deceit
Come seeking solace that we will give
In anointed words which bring healing and relief.

Wounded spirits come fearful hiding
behind a facade
Yet we must encourage them
To open their hearts to us and see God.

In the Holy of Holies as each one is seated
It is our privilege to serve them
Until every unholy thought is defeated.

O, Lord, may we forever humbly submit
To Your will and way
In the Holy of Holies where others come sit.

Benedictions

Womanist Benediction

a ritual responsive reading for the Womanist In-Gathering at the American Academy of Religion

May Alice's Creator fan into flame
Purple-minded masterpieces from the works of our hands.

May Katie's Redeemer wash us again
Purging passivity and renewing our zeal.

May Jackie's Christ atone for our sins
Proving us chosen and called to this work.

May emilie's Spirit compel and encourage us to
Agitate stagnant biblical waters.

May Marcia's Grace liberally flow as we
Perfect our pedagogy and perform our leadership.

May The intercessors' prayers and
The poets' prophecies and
The scholars' revelations and
The sisters' hospitality and
The brothers' solidarity

Make us uniquely one
And aggressively different

Keep us now until we meet again
Immortal and eternal
In the Image of the Divine
In the Power of the Holy
In the Name of Jesus.
Amen. Asé. And so it is.

Dance in Advance

While for that miracle you are sitting and waiting
You toss at night while your heart is breaking
Here's a cure you will find fascinating
just dance in advance!
> *Dance until the miracle comes*
> *to the broken heart, you will not succumb*
> *if you dance in advance.*

While in captivity expecting liberation
While trying to pray through stagnation
Try this out for motivation
just dance in advance.
> *Freedom is only the Great Day away*
> *And God meets you wherever you pray*
> *if you dance in advance.*

If from others you feel isolation
Or if you are plagued by procrastination
Turn to the Power of Inspiration
and dance in advance.
> *It is possible to be alone but not lonely*
> *When each task is consecrated to the One and Only*
> *and you dance in advance.*

Dance in advance of answers and peace
Dance in advance of blessed sweet relief
Dance in advance of seeing to know
Dance in advance because God said it, and it is so!

The Last Time I Preached

The last time I preached
he got happy and she got healed
one water baptized, another filled.

The last time I preached
I was so humbly appointed
and with the Holy Spirit, fully anointed.

The last time I preached
I studied long as a good scholar
but still took my time to 'hoop and holler.

The last time I preached
I stuck to my text from the Word
and others left telling what they had heard.

The last time I preached
I looked forward to the next time
expecting to follow me, wonders and signs.

'Cause the last time I preached
he got happy and she got healed
one water baptized, another filled.

Index

Abba, 169
ableism (see: disabled), 229
abolitionist, 105
abuse, 129, 206
accommodation (see: disabled), 89, 181, 208
addiction, 193
adopt (also, adoption), 159, 169, 193, 223, 224, 227, 228
affirm, 85, 105, 128, 211
affirming (see: LGBTQIA), 45, 164, 212
African (also, Africa), 45, 46, 59, 60, 65, 66, 69, 76, 140, 142, 143, 174, 176, 232–34, 239, 245
African American (see: Black), 71, 76, 143, 155, 232–34
AIDS (see: HIV), 41, 42, 250
Alabama Waterfront Brawl, 65, 171
allies (see: LGBT), 167
All Saints Day, 219, 220
Almighty, 244, 256
Alpha Phi Alpha (see: Divine Nine), 196
America (also, American), 21, 30, 59, 65, 76, 101, 103, 143, 162, 176, 222, 232–34, 250, 265
American Academy of Religion (AAR), 265

Anacostia, 160
ancestor (also, ancestral), 22, 46, 57, 65, 67, 84, 97, 105, 116, 140, 142, 145, 155, 158, 174, 175, 176, 191, 192, 231, 233, 234, 257
Angelou, Maya, 71, 219
anthem, 156, 159
anthropomorphic, 87
anxiety (see: disabled), 23, 103, 253
Asafetida (also, asfiddity), 238, 239
asexual (see: gender), 211
assistive (see: disabled), 43, 181
atheists, 166
Atlantic, 174

baby (also, unborn), 34–36, 59, 67, 97, 98, 121, 133, 219, 238, 253, 257, 259
Baldwin, James, 219
Baltimore, 59
baptism, 37, 38
Barry, Marion, 160
believe (also, believers), 33, 46, 69, 85, 87, 91, 93, 113, 158, 165, 167, 188, 195, 208, 215, 223, 229, 249
Bellevue (see: Ward 8), 250, 256
belonging, 44, 81, 198, 209

beloved, 20, 37, 38, 41, 44, 68, 101,
    158, 168, 171, 209, 211, 220
Beloved Community, 45, 54, 210,
    226
bereaved (also, grief), 41, 99, 101,
    139, 147, 172, 250, 253, 256,
    257
Bethlehem, 29, 30, 31
Big Daddy (nee James Francies, Sr.),
    169, 227
Bill, H.R. 51 (see: DC Statehood),
    105, 106, 213
bi-partisan, 166, 168
birth, 32, 97, 98, 101, 113, 133, 136,
    220, 227, 230, 259
birthright, 72, 172, 182, 208
bisexual (see: gender), 165, 211
black-eyed peas, 175
Black (see: African American), 21,
    57, 59, 60, 65, 67, 69, 97,
    105, 106, 133, 140, 144, 145,
    147, 156, 157, 167, 172, 173,
    175, 191, 192, 195, 196, 219,
    222–24, 230, 242, 257
Black Wall Street, 192
blood, 21, 33, 91, 133, 109, 155, 175,
    193, 221, 250
blood-kin, 227
bloodline, 129, 194
blues, 155, 238
bodies, 21, 59, 69, 98, 128, 147, 172,
    182, 183, 188, 205, 232, 233,
    252, 257, 261
body, 44, 87, 88, 109, 143, 166, 181,
    199, 206, 215, 230, 239, 240,
    245
bombs, 29, 30
books, 63, 65, 71, 72, 172
borders, 23
bread, 63, 123, 145, 169, 220, 242
breast, 65
breast cancer, 203
breath, 30, 69, 81, 109, 136, 138, 205
breathe, 81, 93, 123

broken (also, brokenness), 23, 29,
    63, 81, 87, 88, 109, 131, 182,
    193, 205, 213, 267
broken-hearted, 99, 242, 254
Brown, James, 156
Buffalo Soldiers, 106, 144, 147, 222

Cairo, 142
calling, 48, 87, 88, 128, 249
Calvary (also, Golgatha), 91
Cannon, Katie Geneva (also,
    womanist), 140, 265
Cape, 142
capital campaign (see: stewardship),
    213
Capitol Hill (see: Washington, DC),
    106, 166
CBUCC (see: Covenant Baptist
    United Church of Christ),
    225, 229
cease-fire, 29–31, 240
cheese, gov'ment, 131, 191
Chicago, 101, 162
child (also, childhood), 38, 86, 129,
    134, 158, 169, 171, 203, 209,
    212, 223, 224, 227, 244, 253,
    257
children, 19, 23, 37, 41, 44, 48, 57,
    67, 71, 72, 76, 89, 99, 101,
    116, 128, 145, 148, 160, 172,
    176, 192, 193, 205, 213, 220,
    228, 230, 242, 245
Children's Church, 36
Chocolate City (see: Washington,
    DC), 250
Christmas, 29, 30, 31, 35, 36
cis (see: gender), 165
Civil Rights, 69, 140, 158, 222
Co-Creator (see: Mother-God), 128
code-switch, 209
colonization (also, colonizers), 21,
    76, 169, 232, 233, 249, 261
communal, 59, 230

communion (also: Communion), 19, 63, 67, 69, 89, 109, 111, 128, 129, 136, 139, 140, 193, 203, 219, 220, 256
community (also, communities), 21, 23, 36, 41, 44, 45, 48, 54, 88, 89, 98, 99, 101, 122, 124, 141, 145, 162, 163, 168, 171, 188, 196, 209, 212, 215, 223–26, 233, 250
congregation, 46, 171, 225, 242, 249
Congress (United States), 106, 160
Cooper, Anna Julia, 220
Covenant Baptist United Church of Christ (also, CBUCC), 162, 225, 226, 229, 244
COVID-19 (see: pandemic), 21, 215, 230, 248, 257
created, 44, 57, 59, 65, 67, 69, 77, 101, 130, 136, 138, 198, 209, 212, 226, 253, 259
creation, 32, 63, 75, 104, 113, 139, 244, 252, 253
Creator (see: Co-Creator), 37, 43, 45, 59, 76, 116, 123, 134, 138, 181, 211, 223, 225, 229, 240, 242, 253, 254, 265
crime (also, FBI Index), 23, 101, 162, 238, 245
Cross, 33, 87, 88, 90–93, 139
Crumpler, Rebecca Lee, 219
culture, 59, 76, 89, 156, 175, 197, 198, 219, 252, 257
cure, 230, 238, 240, 250, 267

dancing, 61, 84, 244
daughter, 32, 227, 253
Daughters of Zelophehad, 135, 141, 144, 169, 252
Davis, Miles, 220
DC Statehood (also, Washington, DC), 105, 106, 160, 161
deacons, 140
deaf (see: disabled), 198

death, 33, 59, 69, 90, 91, 93, 99, 103, 104, 112, 113, 149, 171, 215, 220, 240, 242, 257
Delta Sigma Theta (see: Divine Nine), 196
democracy, 105, 160, 222
Democrat, 166, 168
depressed (see: disabled), 103, 104
Diaspora, 66, 140
die, 63, 90, 97, 113, 115, 171, 176, 211
difference, 24, 181, 182, 208
dignity, 44, 144, 147, 148, 160, 174, 188, 205, 222
disabled (also, disabilities), 19, 43, 87, 88, 89, 104, 181, 198, 222, 229
disciple, 91, 109, 111, 116, 169, 213
District of Columbia (see: Washington, DC), 21, 105
diversity, 44, 183, 208, 210, 211
divine (also, divinity), 20, 32, 43, 53, 54, 81, 87, 89, 116, 123, 124, 128, 129, 134, 136, 138, 169, 181, 183, 197, 210, 211, 212, 215, 222
Divine Nine, 133, 196, 197
DNA, 57, 65, 148
Douglass, Frederick, 71, 105, 160
doulas, 97
dream, 29, 54, 57, 71, 72, 97, 143, 160, 171, 176, 195, 197, 209, 219, 221
drums, 46, 174
Dunson, Lisa, 140

earth, 24, 36, 77, 81, 85, 101, 116, 128, 159, 169, 225, 229, 242, 245
Easter (also, Eastertide), 115, 130
Egypt, 59
elders, 46, 172, 175, 176, 192, 193, 209, 211, 215, 225
elections, 257

Elizabeth, Mother of John, 32
Ellington, Duke, 160, 220
embodied, 66, 158, 188
enslaved (see: slavery), 59, 139, 232
entrepreneurs, 65, 247
Epiphany, 35–36
epistles, living, 242
equality (also, equity), 105, 229, 230
erotic, 136
eternally, 48, 91
eternity, 20, 32, 124
Ethiopia, 245
etymology, 133
European settlers (see: colonization), 232
Eve (*the adamah*), 46, 128, 136, 139, 187
expectation (also, expecting), 84, 242

faith, 19, 24, 34, 45–48, 53, 84, 90, 101, 113, 142, 143, 159, 163, 188, 215, 228, 242, 249, 253
faithful (also, faithfulness), 45, 53, 85, 140, 142, 197, 233, 249
families, 23, 29, 36, 45, 99, 101, 145, 147, 159, 162, 223, 224, 225, 227, 245
family (also, framily), 37, 53, 113, 141, 149, 163, 191, 192, 193, 210, 211, 212, 215, 220, 247, 249
family reunion, 191, 194
Father God (see: Mother-God), 187, 254
fathers, 101, 169, 171, 220, 227, 257
fear, 23, 32, 41, 57, 103, 130, 165, 167, 171, 172, 256, 257
feast, 175, 232, 233
fellowship, 85, 104, 249
female, 165, 167, 208, 229
Ferguson, 59
fetishize, 226
fire, 116, 121, 123, 136, 143, 244, 245

first-fruits, 139
First Sunday (see: Communion), 4
Fitzgerald, Ella, 158
flame, 123, 265
Flipper, Henry O., 145
food, 36, 76, 104, 169, 230, 233, 245, 250, 252, 256
footsteps, 130, 174, 205
foot-washing, 85
forgive, 90, 91, 129, 169, 249
framily (see: family), 225, 249
Franklin, Aretha, 156
freedom, 41, 46, 54, 57, 67, 71, 136, 143, 155, 156, 158, 160, 174, 175, 176, 179, 180, 192, 208, 219, 220, 267
friends, 20, 87, 104, 140, 162, 225, 233, 253

gardens, 57, 197
gather, 20, 46, 84, 91, 92, 121–23, 160, 163, 165, 167, 191, 192, 197, 237, 253
gay (see: gender), 165, 167, 250
Gaza, 250
Geechee, 175
gender (see: LGBTQIA), 140, 159, 165, 212, 225, 233, 250
generation, 71, 140
genocide, 30, 232, 240, 242, 244, 257
gentrification (see: colonization), 76, 191, 248, 250
gestation, 136, 259
Gethsemane, 88
Ghana, 252
gifted, 140
girl, 61, 86, 139, 141, 259
glorify, 138, 254
glorious, 33, 212, 214
glory, 32, 61, 83, 106, 116, 191, 210, 211, 214, 229, 230, 251
God-promised, 77
Golgatha (also, Calvary), 91
Good Friday, 93, 109, 112, 121

government, 244, 252
grandmothers, 97, 171, 193, 220
Grant, Jacqueline (also, womanist), 265
gratitude, 195, 227, 233
grave, 33, 69, 76, 101, 147
Great Commandment, 85, 225, 226
Great Migration, 191
Greek, 208, 229
greens, 234
griots, 156
groaning, 103, 142, 232, 240, 257
Gullah, 175
gun, 65, 162, 171, 172

Habari Gani (see: Kwanzaa), 45
Hadassah (also, Esther), 227
Hagar, 139
hair, 136, 220
Haiti, 59
Hamas, 30, 244
Hamer, Fannie Lou, 219
Hampton University (see: HBCU), 195
hands (see: disabled), 198, 199
Hannah, 128
Harrison, LaKeisha, 140
HBCU (Historical Black Colleges and Universities), 160, 195
heal, 98, 99, 122, 147, 172, 193, 194, 207, 210, 222, 230, 242, 253, 256, 269
healing (also, healer), 41, 42, 67, 71, 75, 123, 131, 136, 144, 194, 196, 206, 219, 233, 239, 240, 242, 245, 253, 261
health, 127, 135, 187, 224, 230
healthcare, 41, 215
heart, 32, 33, 42, 103, 113, 115, 122, 187, 193, 212, 225, 229, 234, 240, 245, 259, 267
heartbeat, 67, 123
heaven, 20, 24, 66, 86, 103, 116, 121, 122, 123, 128, 158, 159, 169, 225, 229, 242, 248, 253

herbs, 238
Herod, 142
hetero (see: gender), 250
hip-hop, 156
history, 30, 65, 76, 106, 136, 148, 193, 232, 257
HIV (see: AIDS), 41, 42, 250
holiday, 35, 232, 233, 234
holler, 131, 155, 269
Hollies, Linda, 238
Holy of Holies, 231, 261
homeland, 69, 105
homeless, 21, 129, 244
hope, 22, 24, 34, 36, 41, 42, 45–48, 57, 60, 61,7 7, 85, 91, 93, 113, 115, 123, 141, 155, 158, 160, 162, 163, 171, 192, 203, 204, 215, 229, 233, 240
Hosanna, 83, 84, 111
hospitality, 85, 249, 265
Houston, TX, 130
Howard University (see: HBCU), 160, 195
human, 21, 30, 63, 65, 69, 87, 136, 159, 160, 208, 210, 224, 245, 257
humanity, 45, 59, 85, 88, 97, 164, 234, 240, 244, 247
hunger, 129, 230, 244, 245
hymn, 46, 53, 85, 115

identity, 142, 148, 208, 209, 212, 225
illness, 21, 103, 104, 127, 247
image, 43, 44, 45, 59, 65, 87, 129, 136, 138, 211, 225, 242, 254, 259
imagine, 65, 136, 138, 139, 158, 164, 169, 248
imago Dei, 254
Imani (see: Kwanzaa), 45
immigrants, 23
imprecatory (see: prayer), 232
incarceration (also, prison), 59, 191, 193

include (also, inclusive), 88, 89, 104, 226, 230
independence, 179
Independent, 166, 168
India, 244
indigenous, 105, 233
individual, 101, 121, 163, 230
inequity (see: equality), 59
inherit, 147, 155, 194
instruments, 24, 123, 251
insurrectionist, 76
intercessions (see: prayer), 113, 187, 229, 231
intercessors, 265
invention (also, inventors), 65, 75, 76, 136
invisible (see: disabled), 182
Iota Phi Theta (see: Divine Nine), 196
Israel (also, Israeli), 30, 32, 122, 244, 245
Israelites, 142

Jackson, Mahalia, 220
James, Daniel "Chappie", 145
jazz, 115
Jehosaphat, 101
Jerusalem, 90
Jesus, 19, 20, 31, 35–37, 69, 86–91, 104, 109, 111–13, 122, 138, 139, 142, 158, 163, 169, 198, 208, 213, 228, 231, 241, 247, 248, 251, 253, 266
Jews, 122, 158, 166, 168, 208, 229
Jim Crow, 69
Jordan River, 37, 244
journey, 47, 48, 208, 211, 245, 252
joy, 20, 24, 32, 38, 45, 48, 59, 61, 68, 69, 83, 85, 98, 129, 138, 227, 230, 233, 247
Judas, 111
Judgement, 244
judgment, 104

justice, 21, 42, 48, 54, 76, 77, 88, 97–100, 105, 106, 144, 148, 149, 160, 161, 164, 166, 176, 179, 196, 206, 219, 230, 240, 244, 254

kairos, 45, 48
Kaunda, Kenneth, 142
kill, 63, 162, 203, 204
kin (see family, framily), 85, 211, 227, 233, 247, 252
kindness, 65, 85, 104, 187, 233, 247, 252, 256
kingdom (also, kin'dom), 100, 116, 129, 164
King, Martin Luther Jr., 54, 160, 161, 171
kin'dom (also, kingdom), 122, 169, 242
knowing, 19, 76, 77, 88, 122, 131, 147, 148, 149, 171
knowledge, 19, 71, 72, 97, 195, 213, 230
known, 34, 100, 140, 168, 183, 261
Kwanzaa (see: Habari Gani), 45

labor (see: motherhood), 134, 136, 139
lament (see: prayer), 103, 213, 242, 244
land (also, lands), 29, 57, 63, 122, 128, 144, 159, 191, 242, 245, 252
language, 29, 86, 169, 198, 208, 242, 252
laugh, 67, 172, 194, 203, 230, 259
Lawd, 238, 239
lawlessness, 21, 101
layperson, 46
lead, 36, 53, 76, 105, 140, 144, 169, 249
leaders (also, leadership), 30, 46, 115, 142, 143, 197, 226, 240, 249, 257, 265

276

legacy, 22, 41, 65, 144, 148, 156, 195–97, 211, 230, 234, 250
legalizing marijuana, 59
lesbian (see: gender), 165, 167
LGBTQ, 164, 193
LGBTQI, 158, 159, 167
LGBTQIA, 212
liberation (also, liberator), 59, 65, 71, 135, 142, 143, 158, 175, 205, 232, 254, 267
life, 21, 22, 32, 33, 43, 84, 89, 90, 97, 103, 104, 113, 123, 133, 134, 141, 142, 149, 158, 162, 164, 172, 203, 206, 212, 240, 245
Lilith, 136
liminal, 230
Lincoln, Abraham, 160, 233
locs, 133
lonely, 45, 88, 223, 227, 233, 267
Lord's (Last) Supper (see: Communion), 6, 7
Los Angeles, 101
love, 19, 21, 22, 24, 33, 38, 41–44, 48, 54, 57, 67, 68, 69, 75–77, 85, 90, 99, 101, 104, 109, 113, 115, 122, 123, 128, 129, 134, 138, 148, 158, 159, 163, 164, 166, 168, 169, 174, 182, 187, 191, 192, 194, 198, 199, 203, 205, 206, 211, 212, 223–27, 229, 234, 242, 247, 248, 250, 251, 259, 261
lover, 247, 253
lunch, 76, 86, 213, 222

Magi, 32, 35
magnificence, 135, 253
magnifies, 254
Malcolm X, 219
Mama (also, Motherhood), 67, 130, 131, 133, 227, 239, 259
manslaughter, 101
march, 57, 156, 160, 162, 192, 196, 211

marginalized, 30, 57, 135, 163, 230, 242
marijuana, legalization, 59
marriages, 101
martyr, 69, 142
Mary, Mother of Jesus, 32–34, 128, 139
Mary Magdalene (the Apostle's Apostle), 109, 139
medical, 86, 88, 144, 247
medley, 48
melanated (see: Black), 65, 67, 68, 242
melodies, 57, 155
members, 19, 44, 115, 213, 224, 249
memory (also, memories), 41, 46, 67, 86, 97, 99, 134, 155, 156, 159, 175, 191, 193, 247, 259
menarche, 238
mental illness (see: disabled), 21, 103, 104, 127
mentor, 195, 224, 249
mercy, 21, 29, 30, 41, 76, 86, 88–90, 100, 105, 106, 113, 163, 171, 230, 238, 239, 242, 244, 245, 248, 249, 252
Messiah, 19, 31, 84
metaphysical, 59
midwives, 97, 219
military, 148
Miller, Dorie, 145
minister, 37, 38, 46, 47, 48
miracle, 130, 213, 247, 253, 267
miscarriage (see: motherhood), 238
misogyny, 257
mitochondrial, 65
Mommy (see: motherhood), 133, 134
money, 131, 169, 242
monolithic, 233
Montford Point Marines, 144, 222
Mordecai, 227
Morehouse College (see: HBCU), 195

Morrison, Toni, 71, 219
mortgage, 256
Moses, 160, 227
Mother-God (also, Co-Creator), 113, 165, 167, 169, 187, 227, 254
motherhood, 128, 129, 133, 134, 139
Mothers (also, Mama), 57, 59, 65, 88, 97, 98, 101, 128, 129, 133, 140, 143, 155, 165, 167, 169, 171, 181, 187, 203, 209, 220, 227, 252, -254, 257
mourn (see: bereaved), 59, 99, 100, 101, 158, 164, 233, 244, 247
movements, 69, 226
multi-artistic, 134
Multi-breasted God (also, Shaddai), 129
murder (see: crimes-FBI Index), 59, 101, 225, 226
Murray, Anna "Pauli" Pauline, 140
music, 69, 84, 155–57, 172, 220, 230
Muslims, 158, 166, 168
mystery, 33, 59, 65, 123, 128, 131, 133, 136, 213

naming, 175
nation, 21–23, 29, 48, 57, 63, 101, 105, 121, 129, 144, 145, 166, 208, 227, 240
national, 106, 187, 224, 227, 233, 250
National Cathedral, 250
Negro (see: Black), 46, 175
neighbors, 19, 23, 53, 76, 81, 129, 138, 164, 225, 233, 250, 256
neurodivergent (see: disabled), 43
Nigeria, 245
non-binary (see: gender), 211, 225
non-conforming (see: gender), 140, 225
Norton, Elenor Holmes (see: DC Statehood), 105, 160

Nyerere, Julius, 142

Obama, President Barak H., 162
offering (see: stewardship), 43, 163, 206, 225
okra, 175
Omega Psi Phi (see: Divine Nine), 196
opposers (see: DC Statehood), 105
oppression, 135, 232, 252
Orishas (also, Oshun), 174, 176
out-of-wedlock (see: motherhood), 139
Out on the Hill (LGBTQIA), 91, 165, 166

Palestine, 245, 250
Palestinian, 29, 122, 244
pandemic (see: COVID-19), 21, 187, 230, 257
parents, 145, 223, 227
partisan, 166, 168
pastor, 115, 140, 142, 213, 240, 244
patriarchy, 128, 257
peace (also, peacemaker), 21–24, 38, 48, 76, 77, 99, 100, 145, 158, 159, 164, 172, 196, 199, 207, 229, 230, 242, 244, 245, 247, 250–253
Pendleton, Hadiya, 162
Peninah (see: mother), 128
Pentecost, 121, 122, 123
pets, 166, 168
Pharaoh, 142, 160, 227
Phi Beta Sigma (see: Divine Nine), 196
pilgrims (see: colonization), 232
political, 21, 23, 143, 240
post-quarantine (see: COVID-19), 187
poverty (also, poor), 75, 166, 168, 193, 225, 254,
Powell, Colin, 145

praise, 20, 48, 57, 61, 84, 90, 113, 122, 127, 140, 157, 163, 198, 199, 209, 229, 230
prayer, 21, 34, 37, 41, 42, 46, 61, 67, 84, 87, 93, 99, 105, 106, 115, 122, 128, 129, 143, 145, 149, 155, 163, 169, 172, 181, 187, 199, 205, 213, 224, 227, 237, 238, 239, 240, 242, 244, 245, 256, 247–53, 265
preach, 54, 69, 81, 115, 121, 139, 242, 254, 269
preacher, 122, 140, 163
Presbyterian Church (USA), 140
priests, 142, 244
promise, 128, 145, 204, 222, 223, 231, 240, 244
prophecies, 54, 32, 84, 265
prophet, 142, 156, 158, 219, 244, 247
protest, 21, 77, 106, 115
psalmist, 103, 158
psychiatric therapy (see: disabled), 182
pulpit, 4, 156
Purple, 137, 265

queer (see: gender), 211
queering, 134

race, 21, 46, 63, 233
racism, 229
radically inclusive, 88, 89, 242
rage, 23, 59, 156, 172
rain, 20, 247
rainbow, 163, 208, 211
Rainey, Ma, 155
read (also, read-in), 37, 43, 71, 72, 205, 208, 265
Reagon, Bernice Johnson, 158
Redeemer, 19, 233, 248, 265
renew, 48, 53, 230, 249
repent, 169, 250
Republican, 105, 166, 168
resurrection, 90, 113, 139, 158

revive, 122, 213, 230
rhythm, 155, 156
Riggs, Marcia Y. (also, womanist), 265
Rizpah (see: mothers), 101, 128
ruah, 121

sacred, 81, 86, 97, 116, 147, 148, 156, 160, 171, 174, 176, 181–83, 191, 195, 198, 205, 206, 209–12, 223
sacrifice, 85, 87, 89, 138, 141, 145, 148, 222, 230
safe, 30, 97, 103, 212
salvation, 88, 122, 134, 139, 229, 249
same-gender-loving (see: gender), 159
sanctify, 122, 141, 230, 254
sanctuary, 122, 206, 256
Satan (also, enemy), 102, 111, 112, 261
Savior, 19, 89, 109, 248, 251
scarcity, 23, 233
scholar, 242, 253, 265, 269
school, 35, 59, 76, 101, 129, 171, 220, 230, 259
Scripture
1 Chronicles 4:9. 213
1 John 5:14. 249
1 Peter 1:3. 113
2 Corinthians 5:17. 113
Colossians 3:12. 104
Hebrews 4:14–16. 86
Isaiah 1:17. 206
Isaiah 11:6, 9. 209
Isaiah 43:1. 223
Isaiah 43:18–19. 47
Isaiah 43:4. 205
Isaiah 49:5. 224
Isaiah 61:1. 206
Jeremiah 1:5. 223
Jeremiah 20:14. 103, 104
Jeremiah 29:7. 21
John 11:25–26. 113

Scripture *(cont.)*
  John 13:34. 85
  John 14: 27. 100
  John 14:18. 224
  John 15:11. 85
  John 6:40. 113
  Luke 17:2. 206
  Luke 4:8. 208
  Matthew 3:13–17. 37
  Psalm 133:1. 210
  Psalm 139:13–14. 209
  Psalm 147:3. 99
  Psalm 22:14. 103
  Psalm 23:4. 100
  Psalm 34:18. 99
  Psalm 61:1. 99
  Psalm 68:6. 223
  Psalm 71:9, 18. 209
  Psalm 9:9. 205
  Psalm 91:4. 205
  Revelation 21:4. 99
  Romans 10:9. 113
  Romans 12:1–2. 104
  Romans 8:34. 113
Seacole, Mary, 219
season, 22, 123, 128, 187, 247, 249, 250
segregated, 147, 160
Selah, 89, 188
self-esteem, 104
Senate (United States), 105, 106
Senegal, 142
separate but equal, 59
Serengeti, 59
service, 53, 101, 123, 138, 145, 195, 197, 251
761st Tank Battalion, 144, 222
sexism, 229
Shaddi (also, Multi-Breasted God), 129
shelters, 206
shootings (see: crime, FBI Index), 162
siblings, 42, 198, 211, 226, 227, 250

sick, 250, 256
Sigma Gamma Rho (see: Divine Nine), 196
sign (see: disabled), 68, 75, 181, 182, 198, 199
silence, 33, 54, 93, 148, 182, 198, 199
silent, 29, 100, 176, 203, 204, 240
Simone, Nina, 156, 220
sin, 33, 86, 88,103, 129, 169, 179, 249, 265
sing, 19, 53, 83, 155, 156, 158, 159, 179, 245, 259
slavery (see: enslaved), 69, 192, 208, 229, 232, 257, 191
Smith, Bessie, 155
social media, 45, 88, 224
socialist, 142
solidarity, 158, 159, 162–64, 250, 265
Somalia, 142, 245
song, 20, 32, 35, 47, 57, 67, 83, 85, 115, 122, 156–58, 160, 163, 174, 175, 199, 219, 230, 231
sons, 144, 147, 169
sorrow, 29, 103, 155
soul, 33, 64, 65, 67, 127, 149, 156, 215, 225, 247
Soweto, 61, 63
space, 30, 44, 65, 156, 179, 183, 194, 198, 206, 208, 212, 230
Spelman College (see: HBCU), 195
Spirit, 81, 254
spiritual, 53, 85, 87, 115, 122, 166
spirituals, 46, 155, 175
stewardship (also, capital campaign), 101, 213
stim (see: disabled), 181
stories, 29, 71, 100, 147, 148, 171, 176, 193, 219
stranger, 19, 104, 247, 252
suffer, 30, 75, 100, 104, 233, 240, 247, 256
Sunday, 53, 67, 84, 109, 112, 159, 163, 164, 187, 220, 259
supplication (see: prayer), 229, 231

survival (also, survivor), 59, 61, 65, 155, 162, 165–68, 192, 203, 209, 211, 215
Syria, 244
systemic, 128, 232
systems, 88, 172

tables, 85, 175, 187, 188, 221
tambourine, 84
taxation without representation (see: DC Statehood), 105, 160
teach (also, teachers), 148, 155, 168, 169, 176, 194, 207, 254
technology, 43, 59, 75
temptation, 88, 169
Terrell, Mary Church, 160
terror, 32, 54, 162
testimony (also, testify), 46, 77, 228, 230, 233
Texas, 59, 175
theodicy, 250
theology, 140, 142
Thorpe, Sister Rosetta, 155
Three-in-One (also, Trinity), 123, 124, 254
tincture, 238
tithes (see: stewardship), 213
tongue, 103, 242
Townes, Emilie, 265
traditions, 208, 254
transform, 57, 97, 104, 133, 172, 175, 207, 212, 226, 242
transgender (see: gender), 211, 225
TRANSparenthood (see: motherhood), 134
trauma, 162, 172, 253
tribe, 208
Triumphal Entry, 84, 111
trouble (also, troubled), 24, 46, 100, 103, 205
truth to power, 76, 135, 219
Tubman, Harriet, 219
Tuskegee Airmen, 144, 195, 222
Tutu, Archbishop Desmond, 142
tyranny, 250

Uganda, 245
Ukraine, 244
uncertain, 23, 47, 230, 240
unconstitutional (see: DC Statehood), 105
unemployment, 256
unite, 44, 99, 140, 197, 225, 233
universal, 45, 226
universe, 59, 130
urban renewal (see: gentrification), 191

vaccines, 230, 257
valley, 93, 215, 240
vernacular, 198
veterans, 222
Via Dolorosa, 88
victims, 100, 101, 172
victories (also, victorious), 47, 61, 69, 194
virtual, 19, 121, 122
virus, 230, 247, 250
visible (see: disabled), 182
vision, 43, 54, 105, 142, 172, 197, 209, 213
visitor, 115, 249
voice, 29, 42, 142, 157, 160, 176, 182, 204, 206, 208
vote, 21, 106, 160

wail, 59, 71, 101, 232, 253, 257
wake-up call, 30
walked-on-water, 111
Walker, Alice (also, womanist), 165, 167, 265
walls, 24, 191, 210
war, 23, 65, 160, 222, 230, 237, 244, 245
Ward 8 (also, Ward 7), 22, 76, 182, 250
Washington, DC (see: DC Statehood), 21, 59, 83, 106, 160, 161, 166, 171, 250, 256, 259

Watchnight, 46
water, 32, 33, 37, 54, 57, 63, 65, 101, 103, 122, 128, 130, 143, 155, 174, 176, 187, 225, 238, 245, 252, 265, 269
watermelon, 175
water wells (see: Palestine), 245
weary, 47, 48, 77, 105, 115, 123, 194, 206, 230, 245
weep, 29, 103, 253
welcome, 37, 85, 115, 121, 122, 163, 165–68, 198, 212, 221, 226, 249
West Bank (see: Palestine), 250
white (see: colonization), 21, 167, 230, 257
wholeness, 42, 165–68, 211, 240
whooping cough, 238
Wiley, Christine, 140
Williams, Daniel Hale, 219
Wilson, August, 219
wisdom, 41, 43, 53, 57, 67, 97, 100, 106, 116, 142, 144, 145, 156, 174–76, 187, 192, 198, 209, 212, 213, 215, 219, 230, 240, 242, 249, 250

witness, 84, 98, 105, 109, 121, 162, 163, 229, 231, 250–253, 256
woman (see: women), 65, 97, 136, 138–41, 158, 219
Womanist, 135, 140, 165, 167, 265
Womanist In-Gathering (AAR), 265
womb, 32, 103, 128, 136, 181, 209, 223, 253
wombfruit, 133
women (see: woman), 61, 63, 91, 109, 111, 138–41, 165, 167, 204, 213, 244, 253, 257
workers, 21, 41, 166, 168, 215, 245
worship, 35, 45, 46, 53, 83, 84, 128, 163, 165, 167, 168, 187, 198, 199, 229, 233, 253
worth (also, worthy), 136, 145, 183, 188, 205, 206, 211, 225, 229, 257
wounds, 81, 144, 147, 162, 172, 193, 194, 205, 210, 219, 222, 261

Zelophehad, Daughters of, 135, 141, 144, 169, 252

www.ingramcontent.com/pod-product-compliance
Lightning Source LLC
Chambersburg PA
CBHW060555230426
43670CB00011B/1832